HAMISH BROWN, MBE, is one of Scotland's most revered outdoor writers, ever since his *Hamish's Mountain Walk* told the story of the first-ever climbing all the Munros in a single walk, and on through other stories like the first foot-linking of the highest peaks of Scotland, England, Wales and Ireland (*Hamish's Groats End Walk*) or the first 1,000 mile traverse of Morocco's Atlas Mountains (*The Mountains Look on Marrakech*). World wandering all his life, recent books tell the family saga of the fall of Singapore (*East of West, West of East*) and his two years in the RAF (*Airman Abroad*). He edited two notable mountains poetry anthologies and, more recently some of his best writings have been collected in *Walking the Song* and *Chasing the Dreams.* He has been awarded doctorates from St Andrews University and the Open University and is a popular lecturer. Home most of his life has been on the Fife Coast to which he has now written the definitive guide book.

WALKING BORDERS

In Fife and in Fancies

Hamish Brown

HAMISH BROWN

EVENTISPRESS

A CIP catalogue record for this title is
available from the British Library.

ISBN 978-1-7393286-1-0

Published by Eventispress in 2024
Kinghorn
Scotland

Printed & Bound by Biddles Books Limited
King's Lynn

Even if the doctor does not give you a year, even
if he hesitates about a month, make one brave
push and see what can be accomplished in a week.

Robert Louis Stevenson (RLS)

CONTENTS

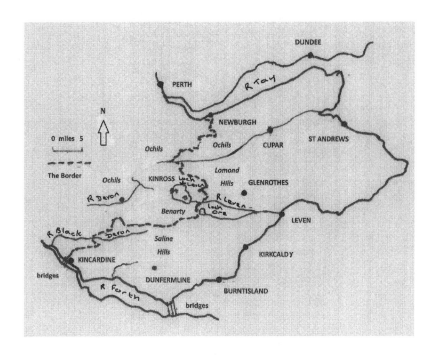

Fife's Border, Hills and Rivers

JUSTIFICATION

I'll to Fife

Macduff; in Shakespeare's *Macbeth*

IN THE SUMMER of 2020, not long after I had walked the entire Fife coast from Kincardine to Newburgh for writing *Exploring the Fife Coastal Path, a Companion Guide* (Birlinn 2021) a friend asked me what sort of daft ploy I would come up with next.

I've often wondered about the science behind the magic of the way ideas just seem to happen; as it did here. I thought, why not complete the bounds of Fife by walking the *overland border* from Kincardine to Newburgh? The first thing I did, once home, was to highlight the line of the border on the Fife maps I possessed, which was a committal, though I didn't realise this at the time. Never mind; when the legs are growing old, it is all the more vital to keep the head young and this would keep legs and head well occupied in the rather fallow autumn of 2020. The very fit could walk the route in three or four days, most push for a week, I took eleven walking days for I was balancing the pleasure of using days of better weather and heeding ,'The thing is to get autumn done, before it gives up contact with the sun'.

The landward boundary of Fife is complex and follows few natural features. In the book I give this Fife Border a capital to differentiate from any other border. Major hills that are ascended are never fully traversed and no rivers are followed for any length. History, rather than geography, set the bounds of Fife, the who –

people – deciding. In the past royalty, nobles, ecclesiastics all grabbed, held and expanded however, wherever they could. As politics is inevitably messy, Fife's contorted border could not be otherwise. Within the bounds, at whatever level, changes continue which adds to the exploratory interest of trying to follow what exists solely on the map. Maps can't keep up. I'm not going to be too particular about following the line; well, I am being particular in not following the line where it does things like running up a section of motorway, or across a loch, or through an industrial site, or along an impenetrable tree-choked gorge or across growing crops. I'll take the nearest common sense possibility, and I'll happily stray to see any nearby feature of interest, natural or manmade.

The way that I went held no compulsions, carried no official 'Way' designation and gave a feeling of genuine exploration. Fife might not be Antarctic or Amazonia but there was plenty to be personally discovered. Wilfred Thesiger wrote, 'No, it is not the goal but the way there that matters, and the harder the way the more worthwhile the journey'. This was quite hard enough for an old man. Walter Hagen expressed my attitude: 'You're only here for a short visit, so don't hurry, don't worry, and be sure to smell the flowers along the way'. I wanted to look for happy happenings and thread myself into a more natural tapestry and gamble awhile with the unpredictability of Scottish autumns. I wanted days of refreshing air which RLS maintained 'the most salutary of all things for both body and mind'.

One interest of this lowly Fife Border is the complete lack of meaning to everyone crossing the line today. But for the road-signs who would notice? Who cares? In practical terms the only difference for people living a hundred yards apart, one on each side of the Border, might be in their council tax assessments. They both would have willowherb, earthworms and sparrows. Nature does not put up these borders. We do. The world is a maze of mankind's borders, all too often lines drawn by war out of greed, or creed, and guns, and now traced by razor wire and walls. Here the course of a burn, a long lost road, the edge of a wood, might be the Border, with nature quite disinterested in the fact, the line simply the result of our quixotic history, any reason lost in centuries past. The very lack of logic, of meaning, in such a line, appealed to me. I would be following a chimera for no forced reason; just to reconnect with that world that does so well without us.

A friend Douglas Fraser once wrote all that I thought and felt.

> Larks trill in the quiet glen.
> The burn skips on the boulders.
> Winds ruffle the smooth ben
> Where sheep browse on its shoulders.
>
> Here have been only nights and days
> Sun and the clouds sailing,
> Moon and stars that went their ways
> And the dusk's soft veiling.
>
> Nothing has changed since time began
> But the slow ebb of the seasons.
> Go your ways, you questing man:
> Life has no need of reasons.

I'm basically a pessimist, which is a good thing for the slings and arrows are then rendered ineffective and life constantly hands out pleasant surprises. Life has no need of reasons; just live, content, within the mystery that is human life.

While much of the Border runs through a rural landscape, a middle portion takes in the historic coal mining heart of Fife, the story of which has always interested me as I was teaching miners' children when the industry died. We don't know when coal as a fuel was discovered (Neanderthals burned coal), which might have been dangerous in ages when the inexplicable could be given devilish connotations. On a pilgrimage to Dunermline at the time of James II, poet and scholar (and later Pope Pius II), Aeneas Silvious Piccolomini noticed the Abbey monks distributing 'black stones', which he had to explain were 'impregnated with inflammable substances' which the recipients could burn at home instead of wood. It would be the Industrial Revolution that made coal – or coal made the Industrial Revolution. And now coal has gone, no more than a comma on the newer pages of the history.

Another matter dictated how the walk was patched together: This was the autumn of 2020 with the odd frustrations of the remaining restrictions. I could not ask a friend to run me to the day's starting points (but alright to travel in a taxi) so, perforce, I had to rely on public transport, often making various changes, to reach any day's starting or finishing point. Some areas simply are not covered by any public services. The logistics were quite a challenge, without any extra complications. The old begrudged the pandemic as much as any. We have limited time left and resented seeing it sucked away fruitlessly.

I'm rather a lazy person and need something to spur me to activity, some committing project ahead rather than just walking for walking's sake, however rewarding are such days. As 'the mill will never grind with water that is past', (Doudney) there has to be some ploy ahead.

This Border walk was done piecemeal, rather than just hoisting a rucksack and tent on my back and heading on day after day simply because I have reached the age of natural decrepitude where such an effort is beyond me. I was setting off in my eighty-sixth year. One doesn't just stop, however moderation is enforced. There can still be a challenge to suit every age and condition and, forget all the analytical guff, we do these things because 'we get a kick out of them'. We have inspiration, motivation, exertion, satisfaction. (The last the rarest quality in too many instances today). Gilbert White in *The Natural History of Selborne* referred to the Sussex Downs as 'that chain of majestic mountains'. That outlook will do fine for my little walk across Fife – and the modest enough hills. Scots tend not to use the word 'mountain' for hills. I once gave away my background in Kenya when seeing Kilimanjaro's summit rise, sunrise pink, above clouds, and gasped, "What a hill!" Someone asked if I was Scottish. How did he guess? "Well, you called it a 'hill'; anyone else would have said 'mountain'".

The walk would accord me a wide variety of meteorological variants, from unseasonable heat, to burly winds, to shrouding mists, to glowering clouds. Each day was an entity, almost a personality, there was always a different setting, type of terrain, engaging with fields, with forests, with hills, and a kiss of sea to start and close. Some days I hardly encountered anyone, other days I was astonished at how many people (and dogs) I did meet. Some days were no more than country rambles but some days, particularly on the heights, were as serious as any mountain venture. Horses for courses. This was what the going was all about: renewing contact with days with only sky overhead and a chosen way ahead. Every day I set off with expectations and every night I returned home tired, sore – and rejoicing. The walk would also reward with the real small pleasures of nature (as against TV's regular overkill).

Fife, historically, seems to have avoided many of the bloody troubles of the Highlands or the Borders. The Romans crossed Fife for tougher matters further north. In early times Fife was the Gaelic *Fiobh* and before that the Pictish *Fib*. Vikings left their marks. England constantly interfered. Perhaps the first folk we'd take as kin would be the Stewarts. They built palaces at Dunfermline and Falkland, the latter offered good boar-hunting, and Mary Queen of Scots played tennis there. Fife's wealth lay in the coastal towns, hence James VI's comment about his kingdom being 'a beggar's mantle fringed with gold'. There were fewer big landowning magnates than elsewhere, so less feuding among the many lesser lairds. Serious drainage work in the 18th and 19th centuries changed the appearance of Fife dramatically and also created 'clearances', more often associated with the Highlands. Fife's most-marked historical period was the Reformation and what followed. A disputatious people we remain. Ferries carried visitors and travellers to Fife but many were heading further north.[1] As one unkind remark I heard noted, "Fife's a good place to live in. It's easy to get out of". Ferries became bridges. Today, Fife is still the 'Kingdom' between the Rivers/Estuaries of Forth and Tay and has character, plenty of character and is an excellent place to live in, appreciate, and explore.

The River Tay's catchment is huge and often noted, but the River Forth not only drains Loch Ard at the foot of Ben Lomond, but takes in the waters of the Trossachs (that not piped to Glasgow for the city's water supply), Loch Voil and Loch Lubnaig. The headwaters of the River Tay have sources from the rivers Fillan and Dochart back to Loch Tay, for the various changing river names back to Loch Tummel and Loch Rannoch, back to Rannoch Moor *west* of the A82 Glencoe road (just five miles from western sea waters). Water is even filched (by Hydro Schemes) from *east* of the A9 Inverness road and fed to Ranoch by Loch Ericht. Angus rivers join in – an incredible catchment area. No wonder the flow into the sea is greater than Thames and Severn combined.

I recall visiting harbourside works in Perth where material scooped up by a dredger was processed and sold as various gravels and aggregates; a very 'green' enterprise before that word became so-used. The supply was endless, the mark on the landscape zero, and Perth harbour was kept operational. This was

1 Queen Victoria with her entourage stopped at the Cowdenbeath change house on her first visit to Scotland in 1842 – and that was about all she did in Fife.

during a school project and one boy, a keen Munroist, turned to me with a handful of gravel and said, in awed tones, "Sur, see this? They chuckies could hae come aw the way frae Ben Lui". Rivers are awesome.

Fife's internal rivers are not quite in the same league as their boundary flows. Only two have any guts: the Eden and the Leven. The former drains from the western Border through Fife's botoxed farmlands, the Howe of Fife, to reach the sea at Guard Bridge, near St Andrews. The latter starts in Kinross-shire's Loch Leven, briefly acting as the Border, and then, through many mills, driving Fife's Victorian industrial economy and entering the sea at Leven. The area between Kincardine and the Cleish Hills is drained by the Black Devon (west into Clackmannanshire before reaching the Forth) and the wandering Bluther Burn (never reaching river status) reaches the Forth near Culross. Rivers were the main source of power in pre-industrial times. Rivers are important. Before the C18 much of Fife was a very mossy, wet, boggy place, only changed by extensive drainage. The same applies to the Forth landscape above Stirling: Flanders Moss. Much of the peat was thrown into the river and washed away to sea, and enriching Fife's shores on the way. Rivers are never static.

Not long after I'd walked this Fife Border I read an account of a walk along the Scotland-England border, Ian Crofton's *Walking the Border* (2014) and smiled at some familiar exasperations he expressed: 'It wasn't till 1778 that the lawyers put the matter to arbitration and fixed the line between Peel Fell and Carter Fell ... After the Kielder Stone the Border jerks crazily about ... Who on earth designed the Border? There's a far better route, along the watershed, without all this dropping down, climbing up, only to drop down again ...' Fife Hills take note.

For me the exasperations were not so much the ups and downs as the irrational longitudinal stabs one authority constantly makes into the other. The Border is as zigzagged as a lightning flash, both in this lowland stretch from Kincardine, and round the void at the head of the Howe of Fife – a void which actually sweeps round to join up with this first one. If a 'better line', historically, never entered anyone's consideration, there must have been scores of debates and arbitrations - and lawyers - to have come up with the nonsense of the Fife Border.

This may seem a very minor challenge, maybe all the more so to someone who has made several hundred-day mountain walks and camping most of the time: the Munros in a single go, the first foot-link between the highest peaks of Scotland, England Wales and Ireland (within the frame of John o' Groats to Lands End) or the complete traverse of Morocco's Atlas Mountains; but that would be missing the point. Everything is relative. And whatever the trip, an integral part is in the planning, the discovering, the finding out afterwards, then writing about it. The Fife Border is only less by comparison but is of the family – a late birth long after other siblings have flown the nest. [2]

I took to roaming the outdoors as a boy in South Africa and, once home to Scotland, the Ochils were a natural lure. One day a

2. I'll note the titles of the books based on these ventures in appendix 1

wee boy decided to climb the most obvious hill he looked at every day from his bedroom window. His planning was rudimentary: shove a 'piece' in the ex-army satchel, grab a staff – and go. The result was pleasing, that first conscious viewing from a high place, looking over what seemed half the world. I hadn't conquered; I'd entered. And have been held by the hills ever since. The roots of this walk go back to those beginnings.

That, for me, then, was challenge enough, Fife's Border, for me, now, will do fine; in between has simply been themes and variations. To all of us comes a time when the limitations of aging worm in and we cannot manage what was once enjoyed. This need not be discouraging. All my life I've said if I were to be so 'damaged' as to make hill-going impossible I would still find life richly rewarding. No one can take in all the world's wonders in a mere lifetime. With aging, the body may say 'No' but one still dreams. 'Old men shall dream dreams' the Bible declares. There may be the thought of a coronary tomorrow but that thought can be kicked into touch, you are much more likely to be knocked down by a car, or murdered or fall down stairs. Life is not to be lived by fears but by up and doing. For me the Fife Border was just such a challenge; being easy or hard mattered not at all.

'How are you?'

'Fine.' (Well, sort of.)

There's nothing so boring as listening to other people's ailments and health problems and I should keep quiet about mine, except I need to mention my physical state in order to justify why tackling this insignificant tramp could be seen as a challenge. You are free to skip the rest of this paragraph. (I won't repeat the list!) A decade ago I had my left hip joint replaced and now the right one is crying out to follow suit. For many years I've developed extreme pains in my toes and the balls of my feet when walking any distance, the cause a mystery to the medics and a misery to me. Two miles of tarmac and I feel as if I'm being 'bastinadoed', walking on fire. (This has been easing off somewhat, after years, and on the Border was not the perpetual penalty expected.) I've a bad left shoulder, a steady pain presence but likely to become a scream in bed at night – as can the right hip, so sleep can be a penance rather than a relief. Ankle joints feel the walking and complain, my left knee now and then just gives up working, my gut is not what it should be and nose and throat suffer a perpetual 'cold' that defies curing, I've weepy eyes and growing deafness. Oh, and I do take a daily clutch of pills following a minor heart attack some years back when two stents were inserted.

On hip replacements, later on, I had a story from the super-walker Dael Wilson, whim I met on the Fife Pilgrim Way. This was about another extreme walker whose left hip was painful enough for him to visit the doctor. He was told he needed a replacement. 'What, just the one? Why not two? The other has done exactly the same!' Dael, I may say, had walked the pilgrim way to Compostela and then 'just' walked home to Fife. When a heavy rucksack became an impossibility he acquired a wee buggy and hiked across France from the Channel to the Med. He had tramped Newburgh to Kincardine on much the same route I followed.

I'm always surprised at the recuperative powers of the human body and a day off after a day walking would see me set up again. I'm lucky: I'm still doing what I like most rather than being incapacitated. Life may become harder with aging but being old is still a much better idea than the alternative. George Borrow, in *Lavengro*, quotes a conversation,

> "A Rommany Chal would wish to live for ever!"
> "In sickness, Jasper?"
> "There's the sun and the stars brother."
> "In blindness, Jasper?"
> "There's the wind on the heath, brother:
> If only I could feel that, I would gladly
> live for ever."

A more cheery observation; many people I encountered in places near to towns were exercising their dogs. Dog owners are quite ready to greet those met along the way but at this time there was only one topic of conversation for people stopping to have a chat and I quickly learned to deflect the inevitable by asking for any dog's name. There could well be a thesis to be written on the choosing of dog's names. Why was a wee hairy mongrel called Hamish? George, at least, had a connection with Joyce Grenfell, Lucy's owner was a Beatles fan, and so on. My mother always suggested dog's names should be chosen with care, one test being, "How would you feel shouting your dog's name at the street door for all to hear?" I thought of that advice when I met one dog called Piddle. There was also a Bramble (prickly teeth as a puppy), Babe (a St Bernard), Dandy (a comic) but most were just from the run of monosyllabic peoples' names. What became very clear was just how important owning a dog was, particularly in the times when not meeting people. Lockdown had not been a let-down for them. I'd a personal dog-names moment once when three of us (hillgoers) were exercising our dogs on the beach at Montrose. Ready to go, we called out at the same time, 'Cloud', 'Misty', 'Storm'.

This walk would keep to lower, more fruitful levels than the Highland hills which would sometimes be glimpsed on looking north. Fife is well garbed in greens. A feature of deserts is their poverty of biodiversity; we have dry, hot equatorial deserts, we have icy, cold, polar ones and in Scotland, in those hills, we have a third, perhaps best called wet. Ours is the only desert created by man though now we threaten all three.

The observant will notice there is no mention of rain in my story. There wasn't any. I made use of all available forecasts to study weather patterns constantly and then grabbed every window when rain would be unlikely. What a difference that made: probably the most important contribution to overall happiness. There were weather tantrums enough through the autumn of 2020, many days when I longed to be on the 'out trail', while rain waltzed down the window panes, the slates on the roof of my flat were tap dancing and I couldn't even see the length of Burntisland's links never mind out to the distant Bass Rock. I had the time, I had the patience.

Ever since reading Stevenson's perfect story *Kidnapped* as a boy I have been an enthusiast, for the man, and his work. (Could someone please remake the film *Kidnapped*, with a better choice for Alan Breck Stewart than Michael Caine). In the months before this trip I re-read all Stevenson's Scottish novels and, since, have been working through his other writings, in particular the accounts of his various, and challenging, foreign journeys, from which I've gleaned matter so much better expressed than any of my own. I am apt to quote RLS.

Fife is always just Fife (or the Kingdom of Fife) but never Fifeshire, no more than you have Caithness-shire, the rule being the -shire is only added when there would be confusion between a town name and -shire name. Perthshire, yes; Sutherlandshire, no.

My route was as likely to run on Clackmannanshire's ground, or Kinross-shire's, or Perthshire's, as on Fife's. I could criss-cross the Border several times in a day. Kinross-shire and Perthshire are now a 'unitary authority' or whatever, but Kinross marks its boundary clearly, on every road, determinedly individualistic. A Fifer can appreciate that. The Fife Border is clearly marked on roads too, 'Welcome to the Kingdom of Fife'.

I find place names fascinating and the margins of my maps often have gems I've spotted scribbled on them. Some of these I'll mention and I'll always give the names that milestone the route, just to savour them *en passant*. The book too is full of comments, reminiscences, wildlife observations, historical notes and soliloquys for which I make no apologies. The tone can swing from a certain playfulness to near despair. I'll happily lapse into a Scots word when it is more expressive than the English and I'm not slow to record the idiocies of this antique walker: laughing at oneself is a very necessary survival tactic. 'He who laughs, lasts' (M.P.

Poole). This was a walk both for legs and for imagination, alternating tease and treat.

Maybe I should have waited for a more congenial season to make the Border stravaig but old men are greedy for the present. I set off to chase the idea before it could perhaps escape. I went alone, for many reasons, and contrary to what is sometimes said, this is both more carefree and safer. Alone, one is much more aware and much more careful, one sees so much more, one makes all the decisions, without discussion or disagreement. On a purely practical matter, I was constantly stopping to look at or make note of things which might not have interested other people, or repeat lore and legend or look at nature's bounty. For instance, Glasgow Cathedrals's founder St Kentigern grew up in Culross under the tutelage of St Serf. Jealous fellow-pupils killed his tame robin but, holy as he was, he was able to bring the bird back to life; or the story in Greek mythology about the competition to find the king of the birds, this being decided by who could fly the highest. Unsurprisingly the eagle soared above all others, but at the point of exhaustion a wren which had hidden in his feathers till then, flew up higher and trilled triumphantly. The wren is Britain's most abundant nesting bird and the one I saw most often on the Border, other than migratory geese flying south.

My feelings about this sort of solitary pilgrimage varies not at all from what Robert Louis Stevenson wrote in an 1876 essay: 'A walking tour should be gone upon alone, because freedom is the essence, because you should be able to stop and go on, and follow this way and that, as the freak takes you; and because you must

25

have your own pace ... and be open to all impressions and let your thoughts take colour from what you see'. In his charming *Travels with a Donkey in the Cevennes* 1879 he writes: 'For my part, I travel not to go anywhere, but to go. I travel for travel's sake. The great affair is to move, to feel the needs and hitches of our life more nearly; to come down off the feather-bed of civilisation, and the globe granite underfoot.' I would also appreciate the flowers seen in a way impossible from a car.

To recap, this walk offered a mix of problems to solve: first finding the Border, then working out a practical route and, finally, physically going and walking the chosen line, with complex travel logistics thrown in for good measure. The Border would not make an official sort of route such as the Fife Coastal Path; however, my descriptions are such that anyone tempted to emulation has something to go on and, with the appropriate maps, no doubt improve my route.

This is not a guide book. Perhaps it is a warning guide: how to keep off the straight and narrow and find problems (and wet feet). I walked for fun but needed the challenge too; after all, the rewards of life come out of challenges, out of the ideas that sparked them in the first place. For a while I escaped 'the Bastile of civilisation' (RLS) to enjoy the soothing simplicities of walking. I have always been a wanderer. For the lifetime of one passport my profession was given as *Gangrel* (wanderer) but I was constantly having to explain the good Scots word at borders, rather difficult, with my limited Cantonese or Arabic. I remain ' – such as cannot use one bed too long, / But must get hence, the same as I 'ave done, / An' go observin' matters till they die' (Kipling).

Maps required

For walking the Fife Border I used both scales of maps: the OS Landranger 58, and Explorer 367 and 370. Annoyingly, both series cut off parts at the beginning of this walk, so for these I just copied the small bits needed from my Landranger 65 and Explorer 366 sheets.

Abbreviations used

C for century, eg. C18 is eighteenth century (1700-1799); OS: Ordnance Survey (maps); WW1 and WW2: World War One, World War Two; FCP: Fife Coastal Path. Sir Walter Scott is mentioned frequently and may just be called Scott and Robert Louis Stevenson is RLS.

Chapter One

KINCARDINE-ON-FORTH

*For the eyes of faith
stones talk, trees sing, the seas dance.
So lend me your eyes.*

The Twa Bridges

KINCARDINE HAS BEEN a lifelong place in my consciousness, for growing up under the Ochils in Dollar (just into neighbouring Clackmannanshire), I often came wheeling into the town as a roaming teenage cyclist. Perhaps, too, my curiosity about place names came from that time. I had once paused at Forest Mill above Kincardine, when a big, swanky American car pulled up and the driver drawled, "Say, boy, am I on the road for Kinkerdene?"

I'd never before considered that a name could be so mismanaged but Fife has a good share of booby trap names. I live in Burntisland which looks clear enough surely; Burnt-island? But no, English people constantly see it as Burntis-land. From Kincardine we look down-estuary to Longannet which is pronounced, with no avian connections, Lon-annat; and a few miles on lies treasured Culross, which is Coo-russ. And how does one cope with Fife's favourite tricky name, Kilconquhar? English people tend to view this pronunciation problem as a singularly Scottish default but England is every bit as provocative; going no further than two names of two syllable, how about Derby and Keswick? (Darby and Kessick; and Kilconquhar is Kinucher).

Most crossings of the Kincardine Bridge, before the opening of the Forth Road Bridge, were made by Edinburgh commuters who knew, exactly, when they would be quicker to go on round by Kincardine than remain in the Queensferry ferry queue. Kincardine Bridge was an unloved necessary evil, but deserved, and deserves better.

Some of Scotland's most historic battles and sieges occurred at Stirling for the geographical reason that that was where, for centuries, the 'lowest bridging point' on the River Forth was situated. Kincardine won the lowest bridging for similar geographical reasons plus the ever-increasing commercial demands, and would hold that lowest bridging position from 1936 – 1964 when even greater pressures led to the Forth Road Bridge being constructed. Modern times also increased the traffic pressure on Kincardine, both bridge and town, so a second bridge was built: The Clackmannanshire Bridge. Oddly, the Clackmannanshire Bridge touches down in Fife – just.

Over the years I have crossed the Kincardine Bridge many times, once, as a boy on a bike, seeing the bridge swivel open to let a ship through. That facility stopped in 1988. Such was the balance that the 1600 tonne swing section only needed a pennyworth of electricity to be set in motion.

More recently I'd come to Kincardine several times when working on *Exploring the Fife Coastal Path*. The Fife Coastal Path had originally run from Forth Bridges to Tay Bridges and, for an earlier guidebook, I made a point of walking into Fife over the Forth Road Bridge and then out of Fife over the Tay Road Bridge (after which I caught a train across the Tay Railway Bridge and the Forth Bridge in turn: a sort of Munro-bagging of bridges). Was a circular walk using Kincardine and Clackmannanshire bridges possible? I rather assumed so, but in the bus began to worry. What if one cannot walk across the Clackmannanshire Bridge?

I arrived in Kincardine after something of a bus tour: Burntisland to Dunfermline to Culross to Kincardine. Buses arrive and depart from Kincardine in an unpretentious, restful village square (High Street). First of all I walked on past the sturdy war memorial and teased a route across the main road junction to Kirk Street opposite. A welcoming wee café, Marco's Kitchen, occupies the basement of the first building, for me, a favoured haven over many visits to the Tulliallan Kirkyard. (Keys for the Kirkyard gate and a descriptive guide can be borrowed from the café.) A bacon roll and a coffee were welcome and two local ladies having their refreshments were able to reassure me that pedestrians could walk across the Clackmannanshire Bridge.

I started my walking from the old market cross (c.1670; the village was made a burgh of barony in 1663), the octagonal shaft topped by the crest of the Earl of Elgin and Kincardine. In those days Kincardine was just 'a small seaport town in Tulliallan parish' (Groome). I crossed a road where looking left was what looked like a church with a rather Frenchified tower with ironwork and a clock. This was the Burgher Chapel originally, one of the many splinter groups of Scottish religion and was built with the main wall curved ('D plan box of 1819' – Gifford). The tower, c1870, was built up against this curve which looks curious. Today it offers a sympathetic residential conversion, something Fife should see happens to derelict churches, factories and shops rather than gobbling up more countryside with expensive developments, which, those most needful, cannot afford.

Crossing, I walked down Keith Street, which I liked at once with its older building styles blending into a harmony. There are outside stairs, many cottage doors opening directly onto the street, red roofs, some larger buildings where windows are in the facing gables, and plenty personalising detail. When Keith Street swings right there are two red-roofed houses, looking very much as they must have in 1734, a date on a marriage lintel for JJ and KS. One is marked The Auld Hoose, a one time pub. Red-roofs were very much a Kincardine feature at one time. Facing these old houses steps lead up to the road as it reaches the Kincardine-on-Forth Bridge.

Keith Street is named after a naval hero, Admiral Sir George Keith-Elphinstone (1746 – 1823), one of Nelson's captains, created Viscount Keith in 1814. He saw service all over the globe: China, India, the American War of Independence, action in the Dutch East Indies and the Capture of Cape Town, then the long years fighting the French, from the time of the Revolution to the fall of Napoleon (he cleared the French out of Egypt). Ship life was a grim grind but he survived, but not to enjoy Tulliallan for long. The only other notable figure born in Kincardine (in the Unicorn Hotel) was the chemist Professor Sir James Dewar FRS (1842 – 1923), who is now chiefly remembered for inventing the thermos flask.

Kincardine receives poor reviews in all the guides I've read which I find a pity. The town has history, has function, has corners and streets with character and, squeezed as it is by busy roads and bridges, remains a calm haven. I hope the Fife Coastal Path will prove beneficial. A B&B would be a boon.

Arriving onto the bridge, a pleasant breeze ruffled my hair – and suddenly, like a door opening, there is a view upriver over the Clackmannanshire Bridge, to the friendly Ochils running along to Dumyat, which some claim RLS saw as Spyglass Hill for *Treasure Island*. This is Kincardine-on-Forth Bridge, to ensure there is no confusion with six other Kincardines in Scotland. The bridge was opened in 1936 by the Conveners of Fife, Clackmannanshire and Stirlingshire. Continuing along the older bridge, coat of arms declares 'County of Fife' and later, looking back, another coat of arms declares 'County of Stirling'.

Counties of course no longer exist. Scotland is now split into Regions (unitary authorities) and the south end of the bridge now touches down into Falkirk – following the big 1975 reshuffle. There was a plan then to divide Fife horizontally and create two new authorities, one based south and north of the River Tay, and the other north and south of the River Forth. The proposal caused outrage and died a deserved death. Tinkering with boundaries has a long history. Fife in earliest times was called Ross (meaning *peninsula)* and extended far to the west, almost to Stirling. There was no Clackmannanshire. Gradually Fife was pushed back and Clackmannanshire created. Kinross gathered itself round Loch Leven, in 1929 linked with Perthshire, and resisted any idea of joining with Fife in 1975 (Fife's higher Council Tax had something to do with it). Kincardine and Culross parishes were for long parts of Perthshire ('detached' the term) till an 1891 shake up.

Kincardine-on-Forth Bridge would never win a beauty prize like the trio at Queensferry but does have an intrinsic rightness for it's task (Category A listed). A guide I read was still somewhat scathing: 'an unexciting lattice steel structure spanning concrete piers, whose approach roads carved up and almost mortally wounded Kincardine.' Kincardine has well recovered but the piers of the old swinging section of bridge now have grass sprouting in the timbers and rust nibbles away generally. One walks with the thunder of traffic. Another plaque notes the bridge's engineer was Sir Alexander Gibb. He was born in Broughty Ferry in 1872. His firm did work on the Barking Power Station, Galloway Hydro Scheme, Guinness Park Royal Brewery, and the British naval base in Singapore.

The bridge stopped being opened for ships for two connected reasons: Alloa harbour closed in 1951 and ships were becoming ever bigger and heavier. The number of ships using the river has declined but the tonnage has soared with the increase of size. I once watched a supertanker inch into the terminal at Braefoot Bay and, though I was on top of the abbey tower on Inchcolm, I found the captain on the tanker's bridge nodding to me, on equal terms.

Seaward from Kincardine the view is dominated by the chunky chimney of the one-time Longannet Power Station which operated from 1969 to 2002. A unique feature was that the coal for generating power was delivered underground, from mines as far off as Solsgirth, 5.5 miles away, making the conveyor the longest such in the world and delivering up to 700 tons of coal per hour. At the moment the Longannet site is being converted by Talgo to build railway rolling stock, so we may see the line round the coast and through Kincardine rejuvenated. I hope the chimney survives, being a friendly old landmark for a big sweep of Scotland.[3] Longannet was Scotland's last coal-fired power station operating, served by the last deep mine in Scotland, which had begun under-the-Forth working towards Airth. Serious flooding was a final *coup de grace*. Scotland has power enough to be self-sufficient; the surplus goes south over the Country Border.

Looking down, I saw a drift of eiders pass under the bridge. One of my favourite birds – and a surprise to see them so far up the Forth. I try to visit the May Island each year and always take a specific path to a specific spot where, right beside the path, I'll see an eider sitting on eggs in a nest of eiderdown. Sitting birds neither budge nor panic so their beauty can really be noted.

In some places they are *coo-doos*, for their voices, in the Northern Isles they are *dunsters*. In those bird-beloved islands birds have a cheery naming of their own. I recall a black guillemot is a *tystie*, a puffin *tammie norie*, a fulmar *maalie*, a great skua *bonxie*, a redshank *watery pleep*, a snipe *horsegowk*. Eider are the most abundant sea duck in the world and, in level flight, the fastest of all.

Where the bridge crosses the south shore is green salt marsh with a wide skirt of tidal mud, a Protected Wildlife Area. A solitary

3 The towering chimney, alas, has been demolished.

cormorant stood in the mud, while on the bank were a group of four herons, one lying down, and further upstream, two more poised sentinels. A group of four large concrete blocks showed where a pylon once stood. With the ex-Kincardine power station on the Fife shore the whole area has a web of pylons.

Kincardine was at one time West Pans (salt pans), and a ferry point, and has been changed out of all recognition by reclamation schemes, schemes made possible by using up the ash spoil from the coal fires at the pans. The smoke and dirt must have been horrendous. The parish was Tulliallan. At one time forty pans operated in the parish. Just west of the Clackmannanshire Bridge we still see the name Kennet Pans.

We soon came to a large roundabout, the signs for which point to a proliferation of motorways: M80, M9, M876, rather indicating a different world south of the Forth and just the M90 heading for Perth over the Clackmannanshire Bridge (and it really slices Fife from the Queensferry bridges). A path cuts the corner and runs along below the approach embankment, then turns under the start of the bridge to give access from the western side. There's a plaque noting a 2009 Saltire Award for civil engineering. The view along under the bridge is gently geometrical with curvaceous patterns receding into the distance. Where would the world be without concrete?

I hurried back under the bridge to spot a curlew I'd heard calling, but there was no sign of one. I might have known. At home, I'd once rushed out into our seaside garden to spot a curlew calling, only to find a starling was producing the call. So it was here. Several birds lined a wreck of fence. The most amazing mimicry by our house starlings was the sound of our garage door being closed. I'd lazily let the bolt scrape across the concrete before it plonked into the hole. This long *scrape-clunk* sound was imitated to perfection, a starling party piece. One of my earliest bird memories (when or where, forgotten) was of a mynah (a bird closely related to starlings) which would render phrases of Hindi to Indian viewers and comments in English to Europeans. Once, motoring across France, I stopped at a Bird Centre in Dombes and came on an identikit party of English prepschool boys observing a mynah. The bird bowed to right and left with repeated, 'Bon jour! Bon jour!' – and a voice piped up, 'Oh, Miss, isn't it clever; it can speak French?'

The view while crossing the Clackmannanshire bridge is wide-sweeping, a long horizon of sky touching earth, the Ochils a greater presence. (Not Ochil Hills, that's tautology). My favourite adjective for those steep-faced, rolling hills is pachydermatous. I know them well, having roamed them through my entire schooldays, and learned hills the way shepherds do, from repeatedly covering the ground, with neither map nor compass. I was never lost, (sometimes mislaid) for if in doubt, any stream could be followed and would bring me down and out, to one of the Hillfoot (*sic*) towns: Dollar, Tillicoultry, Alva, Menstrie.

I paused for a naming of hills: Dumyat (dum-eye-at), Bengengie, Ben Ever, the Nebit, Ben Cleuch (highest, 721m, 2365ft), Andrew Gannel Hill (sounds like a name out of John Buchan), Tarmangie Hill, King's Seat, White Wisp. These are

Lowland names, the Ochils dominate southwards, while behind the range, the Highland Boundary Fault slices across Scotland. The name is old, from *Uchil*, meaning old/tall.

The great hall at Stirling Castle was catching the sun, the Wallace Monument stood clear on its crag, Clackmannan was marked by towers and, bold or secretive, Ben Lomond, Ben Venue and Ben Ledi were having a look in. I was surrounded by the very essence of our lowland landscape: hills and trees, fields and the kindlier hints of man, of small seas and big skies, a harmony so very British. But will this last for we are so careless of our relationship with the earth, man being 'the consumer of the irreplaceable' (Fraser Darling), and still the proud inheritor of the Genesis dictat: 'And God said, let us make man in our image ... and let them have dominion over the fish of the sea, and over the fowl of the air, and over the cattle, and over all the earth, and over every creeping thing ... Be fruitful and multiply and replenish the earth and subdue it; and have dominion over ... every living thing' (Gen. 1:26-28). The only part of that we fail to observe is the replenishing. Did God really mean us to take the fish from the sea to the extent there will soon be no fish? The trouble is that 'man in God's image' has a converse, (if A=B, then B=A) and we have made gods in our endless imaginings, to suit our purposes, to give ourselves the licence to write such destructive words, to demand the obeisance of the natural world and the obedience of other peoples.

We continue to trash the only world we have. 'This planet is not terra firma. It is a delicate flower and it must be cared for. It's lonely. It's small. It's isolated, and there is no resupply. And we are mistreating it.' So wrote Scott Carpenter, US Astronaut. Two centuries earlier astronomer Camille Flammarion warned, 'Men have had the vanity to pretend that the whole of creation was made for them, while in reality the whole creation does not suspect their existence'. Nature naturally keeps a balance. Man has tipped the scales. Worldwide, since 1974, we have lost 50% of our wildlife population and at the same time *our* numbers soar: 1960 a world population of 3 billion; 2014, 7.2 billion; 2050, estimate 9 billion. At what stage does sustainability collapse?

David Attenborough believes 'if we act now, we can put it right. We have one final chance to create the perfect home for ourselves and restore the wonderful world we inherited ... We have time to do what needs to be done, but only if we act now, and move together'. I can't see it happening. We would have to change the very nature of human beings, to eliminate the selfish gene that drives us as *Homo sapiens*. (RLS: 'Bear in mind that man is but a devil weakly fettered by some generous beliefs and impositions.') We, as everything, are heading for extinction eventually, but the sad, mad reality is we seem to be hurrying to that day. Thirty years ago I suggested we were 'a failed species on the way out.' I look in vain for anything to change my mind.

One astonishing, current observation by scientists and geologists, records we are in the start of what they have suggested as the Anthropocene epoch. In unimagined eons ahead there will be a marked stratum in the geological record due to our human presence, our activities, beginning with the Industrial Revolution.

All our emissions and deposits, our chemical and environmental doings have irrevocably disrupted the plant's natural ongoing systems – to that extent. That is some achievement!

But, back to the here and now: the Fife Boundary, the Border. Fife's connection with Clackmannanshire starts at the shore slightly upstream of the bridge and runs over an area almost void of map contours. A rising sea level will redraw the map, but hereabouts man has already altered the shoreline considerably, with new harbours and quays, long embankments, and a ship-building era (early C19 could see a dozen vessels on the stocks), with allied trades: rope making, sail making, and collieries and distilleries. Steamers called on a Stirling to Granton run. Old Tulliallan Castle on it's knoll, well inland, once stood just above the tide line. These were huge changes to the land yet were undertaken centuries before JCB's.

The old Tulliallan Castle, partly ruinous, is not open to the public. It might date back to the time of Edward I (his spelling, Tolyalwyn) and is one of the best preserved type of the Scottish hall-house as against earlier, more defensive towers. Bought in 1798 by Viscount Keith, he then decided to build a mansion, also Tulliallan Castle. A mile north of the town is Kilbagie, which at one time was the largest distillery in Scotland. Burns mentions the place in his boozy poem 'The Jolly Beggars' ('dear' probably refers to price). 'And by that stoup, my faith and houp,/ And by that dear Kilbagie,/ If e'er ye want, or meat is scant/ May I ne'er meet my craigie.)'

Once over the river I was glad to see a footpath passing below and on by an embankment for Kincardine. There was also a bench which made a good place to sit and enjoy both the view and my picnic; a very standard one of oatcakes with cheese and tomato, a jammy piece, and a home-made drink: a spoonful of honey and a squirt of lemon juice, topped up with good Fife tap water, water given first life in the Ochils. This was a very easy day's effort. The miles ahead would take me through, for me, completely unknown territory, much of the way happily lacking main roads, whose walking my poor old feet find so painful. (It is quite difficult to limp on both feet simultaneously.)

With a benign sun and shelter, I spent an hour reading or, more accurately, re-reading one of the few books which still has my Dollar schooldays home address on it. I never travel anywhere without a book to read in odd moments like this, a habit dating back to schooldays. These days I tend to regard such as my 'bus book' and there were certainly buses enough pecking at the Border to have read *War and Peace* twice over, except the choice is usually more lightweight – in literal rather than literary sense. The book was W K Holmes: *Tramping Scottish Hills*, published in 1946, a modest pre WW2 account of exploring Scotland's hills, from his retirement Ochils to the far north, but mainly of hills within striking distance of his Glasgow work place. Re-reading it now I'm astonished at the distance people walked. He was the only adult I ever met, when a boy roaming the Ochils, who became a friend and, I realised later, a mentor. I imbued his all-round interests; not just the doing but the seeing, the feeling, the belonging. He was a fine poet and artist as well. My copy of the book has a postcard of his for bookmark, one of many over early years, commenting on some article I'd written and encouraging my efforts. Apart from when pitches were frozen and teams sent to run up a hill, the school surprisingly made no use of the Ochils.

The path into Kincardine was ruler straight, squeezed between the embankment and a high fence enclosing industrial works of one kind or another, on the site of the once huge power station which closed in 2001. That site had two tall chimneys as if to outdo Longannet. Both of these, and Cockenzie Power Station, were the work of the same firm: Robert Matthew, Johnson-Marshall & Partners. The gathering/distribution of pylons from every direction still dominates the scene. One pylon sits in the sea just offshore, the wires looping across the Forth to a wetland pylon on the other shore. I was there in autumn which slowed the walking down as there were many bramble bushes laden with fruit and my fingers were well-stained before reaching Kincardine.

The straightness of this embankment path is again an indication of how the coastline has been altered. An 1823 scheme saw 152 acres reclaimed westwards and an 1839 scheme, eastwards, reclaimed 214 acres. One sadness I felt was seeing all the various slips and piers bordering the bridge lying unused. Fifty years ago I spent a day of remarkable calm photographing boats of all kinds here. This day there was just one boat anchored offshore. The harbours now active on the Forth are the ones turned into marinas, pleasure craft replacing lost working boats.

I was soon back in the centre of town wondering just how I'd return home to Burntisland. Before even having time to study timetables, a Dundee bus drew in, which took me to Dunfermline, where a number 7 stood ready to go and would drop me off at my door – after an hour circuiting Rosyth and Dalgety Bay. Fife buses never choose to go direct, preferring to go everywhere: a praiseworthy coverage really. I manage a lot of reading on Fife buses. Or snoozing.

Getting Nowhere

There is no foreign land.
It is the traveller only that is foreign.
R.L.S.

Snoozing was to be my undoing the following day. Having departed Dunfermline, the next thing I knew was waking up with the bus leaving the Forth Valley Royal Hospital in Larbert, the next stop Cumbernauld, which must be one of my most unliked places in Scotland. The buses pass below a huge, multi-storied shopping complex, a gloomy tunnel with no easy way to cross from Glasgow-bound side to Kincardine-bound side. In most countries I expect this swap-over would be clearly marked out but not here. The result is being thoroughly mislaid; not lost because eventually, at the end of a passage, one might spot an east-bound buses sign, or one of a dozen people asked, might know where to head. Am I the only person to give himself these experiences? Naturally, under the circumstances, my bladder began to make demands so a search for a toilet became the priority. A couple kindly misdirected me. Signs at a locked loo referred to another on a named street which, without a map, meant absolutely nothing to a stranger. My wanderings ended at some gates leading outside. Maybe there was a shrubbery. I found an Exit but a woman with a child in a pram was there waving at me, trying to enter, so I opened the door for her. I let the door shut and then found I was locked out. Across the car-park was a ginormous Tesco. Saved! My pantomime was over. (A poll in 2005 had Cumbernauld Shopping Centre voted the worst in the country)

This impertinent necessity is one of the curses of aging, often embarrassing in towns and travel but in unwalled miles of country hardly a bother at all, except for some poor insect being near drowned or a beetle scuttling out of range. Just watch out for bramble stems.

I still hadn't found a way across to the Kincardine-direction bus stop. A year before, however, I had been dropped off at that very Tesco, to shop and then cross to that elusive other side to travel home. So, off I went, round Tesco and up to the road (which was fenced off), entered the grim complex's lower plexus, climbed up and found the crossing, and descended correctly to the waiting room beside the sunless road. There was a bus for Kincardine in ten minutes. I finished reading *Tramping Scottish Hills*, but to make sure I was aware of where I was, glanced up at the end of every page. I was struck again by the big days WKH undertook, partly as few people had cars pre-WW2, and there was better public transport. For the Beinn Bheithir (Vair) horseshoe ('a good days outing') he took a steamer from Fort William to Ballachulish, and suggesting walking back to Fort William afterwards. Having climbed Ben More (Crianlarich), he then walked, overnight, to Alexandria (beyond the other end of Loch Lomond). From the hamlet of Lawers WKH travelled all the Lawers Munros and Tarmachan to end at Killin where, after supper, there is an evening stroll before a night on a guest house couch, the only option he was able to find. Can you see a guest house offering that today? Probably against Health and Safety regulations.

On arrival at Kincardine I went straight to Marco's Kitchen for a coffee and bacon roll again. I needed to recover. I set off to walk the Fife Border two hours behind schedule. I hoped this was not going to be typical Border progression. By the end of that day I was doubting the whole project. Out of the café, I turned left up Kirk Street.

Kirk Street is a quite endearing mix of C18/C19 houses, some smartly done up in the C21. There is the modern Tulliallan Primary School on the left then, further on, the double-gabled parish church, 1833. Architect, George Angus. He designed similar kirks for Kinross and Kingskettle. Why waste a good design? I've often thought this about schools, primary schools especially. Why not have them all the same, much of the work prefabricated, and save the money spent on expensive variety? A pupil normally only attends one school after all.

A smaller road leads on to what is named the Woodlea Old Cemetery but, surrounding the church, is really Tulliallan's old kirkyard, one of the most interesting and important in Scotland. In order not to break today's progress I describe something about gravestones in an appendix. This is one that should be visited on more than just a flying visit.

Behind the kirkyard an opening leads into the extensive grounds of Tulliallan Castle, more mansion than castle, and since 1954, Scotland's Police College. The setting is one of immaculate parkland, acres of grass interspersed with mature trees and, thanks to some visionary, younger trees of many interesting species. Walking through the ground was a delight, even under grey skies. Few people were about and only one group of cadets passed round the impressive building. During World War Two this was the home of General Sikorski, leader of the Polish forces in Scotland, whose main task was preparing sea defences against any possible attack.

One of my former pupils when I was a teacher had been a police cadet here, an amiable lad, not obviously athletic, but he won kudos on one occasion during an exercise when a team raced off to try and catch someone acting as a fleeing thief. Becoming, in his own word, puggled, he paused to gain breath and sat on a tree stump. He then noticed that the one being chased was hiding in some bushes, eyes following the misled pursuers, so my young friend was able to make his first (staged) arrest. The race isn't always to the swift. I rounded the building at a distance, heading for the far right corner to pick up what, in the C19, was 'the well-preserved road from Ferry to Dollar, Kinross and Perth'. A startlingly big, well-balanced oak tree stood proud with the Ochils arrayed behind. I saluted what I regard as my home hills. Hugh Haliburton lauded them too, in the C19. 'What hills are like the

Ochil hills?/ - There's none sae green tho' grander./ What rills are like the Ochil rills?/ Nane, nane on earth that wander.'

I walked over to check the oak tree was just that. They can grow massive but rarely so startlingly symmetrical. The old road turned out to be a green path, lined by tree banks of varying depths, with a slope above on which stood Windyhill Farm. There's something about old abandoned tracks; they feel so anchored, they have kindly vibes, as if welcoming a cherished guest. One walks them in silence, but smiling.

I'd passed a brick building by a stream which puzzled me as to the one-time function. I found out later that a waterwheel once stood there and that this was an area of coal pits, all completely gone. One stood where the Windyhill Farm road led off, while south and north of nearby Crosshill were two others. I wonder who recall their names now: Kilbagie, Corsehill, Lady Ann, Oldkirk (the last where the quarry operates today). I thought of the unknown families scattered to – no doubt better lives – all round the world. We are the furthest distributed species on earth. Exodus followed Genesis.

I crossed the road that leads towards the farm, going straight on for more pleasant woodland walking, heading for the Mausoleum shown on the map. One stretch of old pathway was cobbled. I glimpsed the mausoleum up through the trees, but the site was fenced off with a quarry Keep Out sign – yet a gate was provided. First of all I went over a waterlogged hollow of path, which soaked one foot, to climb up to see the Peppermill dam, which is a long, thin stretch of water, the dam itself simply a grass bank. The wind was chopping up the sunless waters so no sign of birdlife, though two swans rowed rhythmically overhead. The superstitious at one time might have seen them as carrying a spirit to the graveyard in the wood nearby. I hurried back up to the mausoleum, the footpath through the gate gouged out by water. The mausoleum was perhaps the most serendipitous encounter of the whole walk.

Graveyards are a long interest of mine. I'd even written a book about them *A Scottish Graveyard Miscellany* (Birlinn 2008) which describes every facet of what can be seen. My main interest was, and is, the fascinating folk art on the stones of the C18. Appendix 2 describes the symbolism shown on stones and lists many other trades like the ones seen here. The first stone on entering shows a skull (a skeleton torso rather) and holding a fine range of the symbols of mortality. There are plenty skull and crossbones, just symbolising death and not, as I was once asked in all seriousness, marking the graves of pirates! Several stones show the sock and coulter (the parts of a plough) for a farmer (and one also has a rhynd, showing the farmer was also a miller), a weaver is shown by a shuttle, and a crown above a hammer is for a hammerman, someone working in metal. The third stone on entering is clearly for a tailor showing his wide-bladed scissors and goose (iron). The earliest stone I noticed was 1697 but most are C18. I then had two surprises. There was one very obvious hogsback stone which is Viking, and at the far rear, there was a row of narrow stones, one with the delineation of a sword just visible, which are from medieval times, possibly Crusader graves.

A convenient tablestone made a good seat for my picnic, the silence only spoilt by periodic noises from the quarry workings just beyond. A robin appeared and duly received a few crumbs. They seem to have humans sussed out. Is this talent inbuilt or learned, after all robins don't live longer than a couple of years? The building is a church though a later cluster of bulky flat stones in the interior show it was, at one stage, used as a mausoleum. As well as the customary old yew tree there were mature specimens of ash, monkey puzzle and pine. I was standing by some birch when a ghosting of long-tailed tits skittered through, some flying mere inches from my nose. On leaving I came on a dead mole; soaking wet so I wondered if it had drowned. The fur had a sheen and the small, paddle feet looked perfect for purpose.

The day went all wrong thereafter. With the quarry workings ahead there was no way through to Tulliallan Farm but, back a bit an old bridge was almost certainly the line of the old road and the 25,000 map did show a continuation. I tried to continue but the going became more and more jungly and wet (I soaked the other foot). Fallen trees, rhododendrons, brambles, nettles (which stung through my trousers) and rosebay willowherb made a malevolent mix. I spent an hour on this jungle warfare before admitting Time had lost the road through the wood. The only reward was looking at one animal track and speculating badger then, at once, coming on a big bank of sandy soil which proved to be one of the largest badger setts I've ever seen. Thinking about nettles, my plant lore book has several entries by people recording their gathering of nettles in large quantities during WW2. These were spread to dry and then bundled off as directed. Why they were wanted was not explained. Any reader know? During WW2 the Singer factory in Clydebank was largely destroyed by German bombing and the resulting spread of rosebay willowherb came to be called Singer weed. The rhoddie here was the maligned *R.ponticum* which spreads often to the detriment of native species. I recall laughing aloud (at quite the wrong place) during a screening of the film *Rob Roy* for, in the background, was a showy spread of various rhoddies – which in Rob Roy's time had not been discovered.

My retreat took me back to the junction I'd passed. Turning right and, one field on, right again led to a parallel route for Tulliallan Farm – I hoped – clear enough on the map. Tulliallan golf course lay on my left and, on the right, I passed Crosshill.

Crosshill appeared to be an old farm converted to a modern home and garden, the garden crowded with every idea from catalogues or watching garden makeovers on TV. The way ahead was a green carpet of subdued grass. (After all it was an old drove route). Alas, the track soon began to grow wilder and wilder till progress was again impossible; shaking and sweaty, I picked handfuls of brambles while waiting for a quartet of golfers to tee off on the other side of the hedge. Bursting out on them might have been interesting. I wonder what they thought I was up to thereafter, stuttering along behind them, papers in hand (the maps) looking down into a jungly dell. I was still hoping for a way through. Damn it! Tulliallan Farm was only 300 yards away. I tried to use the many power lines visible for navigation but could make no sense of them. Soon I could make no sense of anything. Barring progress down in what was now a steep den was a long pool. The golf course still ran on past it which didn't agree with the map. Had they extended the course? I could make no sense of tree plantations on the map. In the end I sat under a clump of birch to force some sanity into proceedings and regain 'the calm that nature breathes' (Wordsworth). I desperately needed some sustenance too. A kestrel was working the edge of the golf course with enviable ease: hovering then swinging away, hovering and swinging away. In ten minutes of half watching I did not see it dive on any prey. Scientists have shown the tip of the bird's beak moving less than quarter of an inch during a minute of hovering. In Orkney the kestrel is *wind-cuffer*, in Shetland *moosie-hawk* – and the bird is the expressive *windhover* of the Gerard Manley Hopkins poem.

I was once walking down from Derry Lodge to the Linn O' Dee with a school party when we caught up with a friend stumping along with his big staff; one Syd Scroggie. He was blind and had an artificial leg. At once Syd pointed to some deer grazing down by the burn and then cried, "And look there. See the kestrel". The lads were open-mouthed, but he explained you made fewer identity errors with birds when you only had your ears. "Learn to use them." Syd had been blown up near the end of WW2 but was determined he would return to his much loved Cairngorms. I first met him on top of Lochnagar when he pointed out all the things we could, and should, see. Nobody had the heart to say we stood in blowing cloud and saw very little. When I knew him better I told him about this incident knowing it would just get a guffaw. I followed Syd's advice and didn't listen to music as I rambled. "Leave listening to music to the deprived urban jogger. Nature has its own better music." This was not advice I always followed. I can recall one occasion when a school group, having traversed all the Munros between Glen Lyon and Loch Rannoch faced a two hour road walk back to base at Garth Youth hostel and they sang the whole way without any repetition, from Verdi choruses, to our own words to hymn tunes, to the latest pop. There was one break, as a big rock-held, black-water pool was irresistible, and better still, we returned thereafter with supper hidden in a rucksack.

From my shady spot I could hear traffic off right which could only be on the A977 inland from Kincardine. I had followed the golf course edge from going north to near south west without noticing. I didn't find this incredible. I recalled something akin on the winter-hills above Glen Feshie when two of us were aiming for a peak that came and went ahead on the cloud-blowing plateau. Eventually we had to take a bearing but when we came on footprints decided we could just follow them, which we did. Our two prints soon became four. In no time at all we caught up with more prints and the penny dropped. We were circling on our own track but with no hint of this even though the circle was small. So bending, unbeknown, round the golf course edge was quite easy. I'd not brought a compass, not for just following map-clear tracks. Before any third navigational ambush could occur I decided the best course was to abandon these back-lands and head home. Sadly, by the time I'd walked the rest of the golf course, and police policies, and Kirk Street, Marco's Kitchen had closed. I was too weary to read my bus book and slept most of the way to Dunfermline on the bus. Dunfermline was the terminus or heaven knows where I'd have woken up.

This falling asleep is not entirely a phenomenon affecting oldies only. I'd an unforgettable experience as a teenager. I was holidaying with the family in Crail and set off to cycle to Blair Atholl to join a Schoolboys' camp. There was a ferocious gale from the west and I gave up, exhausted, at Cupar, and opted for a train. I'd change trains at Ladybank for Perth and, hopefully manage to cycle the rest of the way. Those were the days of guards and guard vans and my cycle was duly transferred for Perth but I, however, woke up in Kirkcaldy, having missed Ladybank where I should have changed trains. Some hours later I duly collected my cycle from where it was held in a faraway storeroom at the end of a platform, and Perth station had – has – very long platforms.

There are 42 Royal Burghs and Burghs of Barony (our historic towns) in Fife, but only two are on the Border and they mark its extremities: Kincardine and Newburgh. Maps, pre mid-C18, showing roads across Fife were quite blank west of the Inverkeithing – Kinross Great North Road. That night I would designate this area the 'Void of Fife'. Would I ever escape Kincardine?

> It is on etched hills and lithoid seas
> That the stars appear to spin free
> About the sky. Freedom is a glance
> At the wheeling stars and we
> Find that sight by choice, not chance

And what's the proverb about, 'as you make your bed, so you must lie upon it'? My Border walk could only improve.

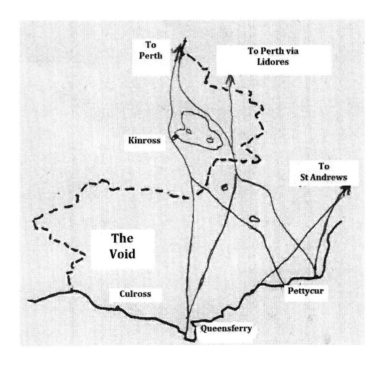

Early Roads on Pre-1750 Map

Chapter Two

THE VOID OF FIFE

Autumn's last dancing,
After which colours find rest
And leaves find sleep.

Serendipity Country

MY EARLIEST MOUNTAIN memory is of my parents climbing Mount Fuji in Japan on the day World War Two broke out. I cried my eyes out at not going with them. Was this my awaking moment of wanting to be out there, up there?

Fifteen months later we were fleeing the Japanese invasion and the fall of Singapore, to spend time in South Africa before returning to Scotland towards the end of the war. In South Africa I roamed with Zulu friends in a place with the evocative name, The Valley of a Thousand Hills.

We settled in the small town of Dollar, which snuggles below the Ochils, hills which were seldom out of sight on this Border walk. The whole family were great readers and, even as a teenager, I would never go anywhere without a book in my pocket or rucksack. I still don't.

The next 'bus book' I chose was the thinnest Penguin on a big shelf of fiction waiting to be read 'someday'. I removed the 49p charity shop sticker and shoved the book in my rucksack. The man-eaters of the title had caught my attention: *The Man-Eaters of Malgudi* but I'd really bought it because of another connection.

One of my top-favourite books, read again and again, is Jim Corbett's *Man-Eaters of Kumaon*, his story of dealing with these dreaded miscreants, some of whom killed hundreds of people and terrified whole districts. Corbett's book is not the work of a gung-ho trophy hunter but gives his sensitive feelings for the jungles. (He first roamed them as a boy with an old blunderbuss and would happily fall asleep and wake to find tiger paw marks had been left at his side.) There was also a family connection because the book first appeared in India (1944) and our father, working in Calcutta, sent a copy home to us. The book has never been out of print since. *Malgudi*, I discovered, was a big fictional Indian city, the setting for a whole series of Narayan novels (published pre WW2), describing Indian life as no outsider could do, in a style, warm and sometimes very funny. I liked the book at once. Reading at least kept me awake on the buses back to Kincardine.

No messing about. I reached Tulliallan Farm up a drive from the A977 main road north out of Kincardine. The map gave the entrance lodge the name Moss and there were plenty of those on the map, as well as muir, carse, ford and pool to suggest something of the landscape to cross on this least known part of Fife. The drive however was lined with fine lime trees and, in the gaps, junior specimens had been planted and surrounded with lifestock-proof barriers – all rather posh for a farm track to a quarry. Surely there was a mansion? And so there was, set behind a high, curving wall, and declaring 'Tillicoultry Quarries'. Big barns of the farm lay beyond, and the quarry on again. The mausoleum could only have been a few hundred yards away but the old north road had been quite obliterated.

There were signs of an old route behind the farm: a sunken, green way between walls, but thereafter just a path through a wood. The entrance to the wood was marked by a solitary, oddly, ahead-of-schedule birch tree in full gold, like a flame against the conifers. I like old ways: they whisper; modern 'made' ways shout. The woods were pleasantly cool, walker friendly; on freezing days they are warm, on hot days, they are cool. Dickson's Wood. There were saucer-size toadstools of post-box red. Sadly, there was a half-eaten baby hedgehog (for once, not car kill). A thinned area had Scots pines straight as masts, the world's most widely distributed of pines despite the name. The tree mix however was all-inclusive. I picked up conkers and beech mast, prickly Spanish chestnuts and acorns, some of which I pocketed to try and germinate (another life-long habit). I was an enthusiastic conkers player as a boy and knew every tree near Dollar where I could gain my conkers, my hoped-for hundreders.

When more open ground was gained and shorn fields covered the gentle billow of hill, there was a sharp view, like a Van Ruysdael painting, of distant Clackmannan, glowing reddish-brown with golden highlights in the sun, the church tower rising in the midst and the castle on top of King's Seat Hill, a fine culmination of my view. The view *from* Clackmannan Tower is one of the Lowland's best in Scotland. Dumyat was shapely, above the pencil stroke of Wallace Monument and bigger hills lying hazily beyond; one, Ben Ledi, was climbed by Queen Victoria; so she was into Corbetts as well as Munros.

Various stories are told about Clackmannan. King David I did grant a cousin Robert Bruce the barony of Clackmannan in 1359 and a Mrs Bruce of Clackmannan (1701-1796), a zealous Jacobite, used the family heirloom sword of King Robert the Bruce to 'knight' the poet Robert Burns in 1787. I was fascinated as a boy by the derivation of Clackmannan (clack meaning *stone* and mannan meaning *glove*) but the story sounds far-fetched. King Robert the Bruce staying at the tower, on leaving, left a glove on the stone and when he discovered this he sent a servant back to fetch it. The servant commented, "If ye'll just look aboot ye, I'll be back wi't directly" – and so he was, with the glove. Well, the county motto is 'Look Aboot Ye' and there is a venerated boulder on which the glove was left – a boulder which has much more interest as having pagan importance a thousand years earlier. The stone now sits, three parts cemented together, on a high stone shard to keep it safe, beside the town's tolbooth and market cross in the heart of the charming old town centre.

The A907 Alloa – Dunfermline road came as a shock, but I did have walkable verges, and I was only on it for ten minutes. I could have filled respective bins with tin, glass and paper in that time, the casual litter of motorists. But worse was to come; over the miles ahead, miles of quiet beauty, I came on the contents of a stripped kitchen at a field gate, a washing machine in one ditch, a mattress in another, and a wooded edge glittering with smashed bottles. And much more of the same. I find this is baffling. Why such a callous disregard for the only world we have? Every town has bins for just such items (recyclable too) yet the junk is taken miles and miles by car to be dumped. Sadly, we have with us those who cannot look on things lovely but must befoul them.

For years I have regularly cleared rubbish dumped at a woodland layby near my Burntisland home. Once I came on a man at the layby struggling to haul something out of the car boot. He saw me and at once gave over, jumped in to the driver's seat and hurried off. The worst ever mess at that spot was finding a complete pile of kitchen material, including all the cardboard, polystyrene, plastic packaging for what was being installed at home. Some of this gave an address – in East Lothian. Hence they, whoever, had piled everything into a vehicle, probably drove past their local dump, went through or round Edinburgh, crossed the Forth and followed the coast till chancing on this spot. Clearing that lot was beyond me so the council had a call. Having the lout's address, I had an idea: a computer savvy friend devised an impressive letterhead for a fictitious environmental society and we wrote the culprits a stinker, ending that we had reported the incident to their local authority and the police and they could look forward to a hefty fine or court appearance. It seemed the best I could do.

Slack Cottage was passed, the walls blasted back to the original fine stonework, new red tiles on the roof, and much else being done; a salving scene which was repeated on two more occasions – as heartening as the fly-tipping depressed. There are still a few more near-ruins that could be resuscitated. A bridge surprised me for it spanned a road not a river. That was not on my map and then there was a car-park beside this road, noting various national cycle route numbers, west to Clackmannan, Alloa, Stirling, east to Blairhall, Oakley and Dunfermline. My map was an old one and, replaced, the new map clearly showed these cycle ways were using a one-time railway line from Stirling to Dunfermline. The route passes the one-time Devilla Sand Quarry, a huge area with plantations and lochans shown. The northern edge of this site is the Bluther Burn which the Border follows in one of a few logical stretches, but then doubles back for no visible reason. I'd wondered if I could use the burn or cycle tracks but that led to several *moss* names and then the problem of making north through farmland. (The cycleway soon went too far off the Border to be of use). I decided to play safe and keep heading north, making a base line across this Clackmannanshire map arrowhead line into Fife. My road did have regular 30 m.p.h. signs, Walking and Cycling Friendly Road.

Brucefield House lay to the west, well-hidden, with glimpses of ponds and walled garden, and probably the reason for the rich and varied road verge trees. The road frequently had ditches of black water alongside, overhung by hard ferns, and ungetatable brambles. I found a patch of cyclamen in bud, and several stretches of aster and tall sedum – all presumably garden escapes. At Red Yetts, another cottage being renovated, I stopped for my picnic. Sun and shadow had been playing tig all day. I was relishing a landscape (despite the tarmac) which, though farmed, had a roughness, a sparseness, a world hard won, not fully subjugated, and still garbed in the subtleties of country colours.

Earlier I had seen a red squirrel scampering about on the ground in a dark woodland and, now, in more open country, I was able to watch a kestrel. I caught sight of the bird taking off and watched it looking over the fields, then hovering several times before flying behind School Wood. Another wood clump was loud with rooks, both in it, and in erratic displays above. The best sighting of the day was a tree-creeper, on a Scots pine, just over the ditch: a movement caught my eye and I watched the undressy bird dart round the trunk and play peek-a-boo as it worked upwards. A wren darted across the road. A blackbird scuttled through the jungly verge and the voices of great tits came down from on high. This somewhat untidy landscape was a good one for the little ones of the hedgerows. As I sat nibbling my jam roll a chaffinch was quietly searching among the leaves for nourishment. Two joiners, working on the house, sat in their van no doubt enjoying their pieces too.

I was rather dreading the penultimate length of road which was drawn across the map, west-east, in almost a straight line, but there were slight bends, enough never to give the disheartening view of road going on and on for ever. The Ochils had strangely sunk to view as I gained height but now, walking on what was a rolling plateau, they stood out boldly. Castle Campbell, above Dollar, was on eye level. A nearer horizon was the sterile workings of a once opencast coal mine, a huge area moated by the Black Devon. A roadside sign: Welcome to the Kingdom of Fife.

Piperpool; house, plantation and Moss were in Fife. The Piperpool name is on Roy's map of 1753. This higher ground was drier and more prosperous-looking. Ahead loomed the tidy-looking Saline Hills, the masts on the Knock just showing.

My feet were feeling about ready to combust so I crept under some ash trees, took off my trainers and lay back for half an hour with a fine feeling of relaxation. Even though I live 56 steps up, with a view over green links, sands, and estuary, out to the Bass Rock, there is the cloying presence of the urban: a palette lorry grinds past, the pipe band are being tutored, a train runs by, dogs are yapping, and a huddle of girls in the shelter of the toilet block are smoking and practising obscenities. (I sympathise with them, growing up is hell – but so is growing old.) Here there were no sounds made by humans and very few sounds at all. A Sainsbury's van had been leapfrogging me and now passed for a last time. This stretch of road was the Forestry Commission's Cadgerwood, the big house named Cadgerford (a *cadger* being a pedlar). A honeysuckle adorned bushes beside me and a last few flowers still gave their heady scent. Honeysuckle was one flower which people thought gave bad luck if taken indoors. Others I can think of with the same prohibition are ivy, blackthorn, hawthorn, gorse, bluebells, lilac, snowdrops (and broom in the month of May).

As boys we just seemed to absorb rural knowledge and on any youthful ramble I'd return with hazelnuts, watercress, elder flowers or berries, and during the day would have guzzled wild strawberries and raspberries and sucked nectar out of clover. There were also the items not to be eaten and, from ignorance then, I never learned about mushrooms. We had six hens and four beehives in the garden and grew vegetables. The war made us much more aware of the natural world. I was allowed to create my own garden and, marked out by stones, I was a bit peeved when someone commented it looked (quite correctly) like a well-dressed grave. But that is how we learn.

While I lay there a minute fly landed on the back of my left hand and remained at rest. I was able to produce my 10x magnifier to look at the tiny thing, smaller than the traditional pinhead but nevertheless perfect, with transparent wings and gleaming eyes. Beautiful. How could you weigh such a wisp of life? My marvelling was then given a jolt as I watched this little nothing shoot out a whatever to stab it into my thick skin. I felt the stab, winced, and shook off the fly in automatic reaction, then itched for the next hour. The fly may have been next to nothing but punched far above its weight.

Coincidences are life's happiest ambushes. That night, as I sometimes do, I opened an anthology at random to ease bedtime and there was William Blake's 'The Fly', which ends 'Then am I/ A happy fly./ If I live/ Or if I die'. I always carry the magnifier in my pocket to look at nature's micro world, mostly lichens (insects seldom sit still long enough to study) which are a perpetual wonder. Even the commonest flower (like knapweed say) under the magnifier revealed secret satisfactions; the mathematical rightness seen in flowers is marvellous. As a teenager I tried to make dyes from lichens, being first fascinated by the gaudy yellow species on the seaside rocks in the Western Isles. I boiled up everything imaginable but the interest was banned when I dropped some wax into a boiling rhododendron flower mix and the concoction went bang, sending a pillar of flame to the ceiling. Photographing what I call natural abstracts is much safer, whether lifesize or micro. Not so long ago I was leaning my head on my arms looking closely at lichens on a wall next to a bus stop in Aberdour when a matronly lady patted my shoulder to see if I was alright. "I thought yous wis greetin."

Ah well, trainers on again; I set off feeling well-refreshed. I met nobody on foot this day and only a couple of cyclists overtook me, their sudden voices, behind, startling, then brief hellos and I watched them stand on their pedals as the lang stracht got to them. The B913 Saline to Dollar road came sooner than expected, and was to be unpleasantly busy. Walk a field edge or two? Signs on the fence warned, Deep Water for an innocent looking marsh. Then came a real serendipity moment. Saline Shaw notices declaimed: Estate Office, farmer's shop and café! (The exclamation mark is mine.) Hands washed, I was soon sitting enjoying a cup o' kindness (just coffee) and a brownie, the perfect boost before the day's last long mile. Everything looked new. Young rowans and other species had been planted round the site but space had been left so the view to the Ochils was uninterrupted.

"How long have you been open?" I asked.

"One month."

The café was surprisingly busy. I wasn't the only escapee. The conversation was all about how life had been so inconvenient. A woman, perhaps in her forties, suggested to her older companion (mother?) that this must remind her of the war. The response was sharp: coronavirus had just been an interruption of indulgent living, the war a long sadness; rationing, blackouts, bombs, and one breathed death. I felt quite guilty! Someone else produced the cheery thought that someday we might have a far deadlier pandemic – and how would we cope then? I almost wanted to yell some rebuke. "Get out there and make contact with reality!" (They had all arrived by car.) I couldn't resist a chunk of cake when paying the cheery lass at the till. A needed restorative, I kidded myself.

Walking on I came to Black Devon Bridge, whose waters spring from the Cleish Hills and wend through the 'wee coonty', to encircle Clackmannan's island setting, create the 'Black Devon Wetlands' and finally wiggle through the stark farmland reclaimed from the sea, to enter the River Forth's original gathering of hill streams forms the Nettly Burn, which becomes the Black Devon at Outh Bridge.

Shortly after passing West Saline Farm I crossed Lilly's Bridge (over a burn which immediately joined the Black Devon). In earlier times Black Devon was sometimes shown as Little Devon. From here down to Piperpool the Black Devon was the Border. In the other direction the Border went off from Lilly's Bridge to go up the wood-enclosed Roughcleugh Burn to near Tethyknowe before starting the circuit of Cult Hill. I decided there was no hope of following this, so I rang for my transport and walked on up the B913 to the agreed pick-up point, where I waited twenty minutes.

It was long enough to feel sad at not simply finding some nook where I could pitch a tiny tent or bivy, cook a rewarding meal, write up the day, read, and sleep below stars, something I had always done on other ploys that could sometimes last months not days. Such travels became lifestyles in themselves, these were days breaking free of an altogether too busy home way of life. Still, the days waiting for the next good weather, simply made the escapes, when they came, more vital. The old as well as the young still thirst for life's experiences. We cannot rest old hungry hearts.

> I am a part of all that I have met;
> Yet all experience is an arch where thro'
> Gleams that untravelled world, whose margins fade
> For ever and forever as I move.
> Tennyson: *Ulysses*

The thing is to keep moving, to remain dog curious. "The old man with a hideous yellow rucksack" was duly found, the taxi cut over to the thundering A77 and purred down to Kincardine. I crossed the road at once to board a bus to Dunfermline, where I'd only five minutes to wait for the bus home (which takes an hour, so I buried myself in my book). The day had been a pleasant surprise. I seemed to have walked with friendly trees and gentle views all day.

Inland from the Forth, up to the Cleish Hills and spilling into both Clackmannanshire and Kinross-shire is an area in which maps show far fewer main roads than elsewhere, an area somehow neglected by the big deeds of history and feeling quite different to any other part of Fife. At Lilly's Bridge I crossed into Clackmannanshire and, on the morrow, will dodge into Perth and

Kinross briefly, before returning to Fife, to find my way out of this Void of Fife.

Towards Cult Hill

The lover of mountains must go to the mountains,
otherwise he will cease to be a person...
and he will lose the very joy of life.
Kurt Diemberger.

The return was a surprise, partly because this was not the next day, but over two weeks later, when autumn had been racing through with my walking the other sections, day by day, to Newburgh, which had been possible by public transport. A change in current rules now meant I could reach this previously unreachable area and walk the last two missed out days.

Coastal Fife had been clear on leaving home but, on gaining the height of inland Fife, we ran into dense mist. "The car's saying 4° and possible icing." Mist had been forecast and would clear later – maybe. (I was always amused listening to forecasts in Morocco: they all hedged their bets by ending "Insh' Allah", *God willing*.) Being dropped off in the void was quite a jolt. A heap of old dung in the nearest field was covered in thistles and umbellifers which were festooned with jewelled cobwebs. Later I tried wiggling webs with a grass stem but no spiders came to investigate a possible catch. I was cold and strode out to warm up, for the quarter of a mile in Clackmannanshire. Then I turned off at Solsgirth into Perth and Kinross, at a field holding emus.

Solsgirth at one time had a colliery and there were plans to link with the mine at Dollar but the geology was too complex. Solsgirth was, however, shipping coal to Kincardine – underground. Geology, the land, has always influenced us, and we it, so slightly. In the words of Hugh MacDiarmid, 'What happens to us/ Is irrelevant to the world's geology/ But what happens to the world's geology/ Is not irrelevant to us.'

But back to the emus. There were two adults in a field who stalked over to greet me, making low-pitched sounds reminiscent of bitterns, and in a second field one gawky young one, along with a teenager. The Cadger Burn ran past and off left, through overgrown woods, lay Solsgirth House (in scaffolding), while, right, was tidy Solsgirth Home Farm. A sign in a triangle said, 'Slow. Hedgehogs.' I didn't see any, but the day was notable for not seeing anything that had been flattened by a vehicle, well, not till the A823 when I noticed the tatty remains of a roe deer on the verge. What was different today was having the road edged with trees almost continuously, sometimes in thicker bands, while large or small woods lay half-hidden everywhere. Fields were smaller than in the Howe of Fife and the ground being much soggier, largely given over to grazing rather than crops.

At Gateside I was welcomed by clucking hens and a brazen cockerel crowing. Signs there, and at all junctions (Fossaway Cycle Network), amused me by having Saline's distance continually varying and at one junction Saline was indicated in two opposite directions. Along by cottages was a length of colourful beech hedging, patched in every tone of leaf, yet eventually all will turn into the rich brown of winter beech hedges. I've always puzzled why beech hedges keep their leaves right through winter when beech trees drop theirs like any other deciduous species. To date the scientists can only reply to questioning with a sorry 'The mechanism of leaf fall is still not yet fully understood'. One reason I'd like to live for a few more decades is to see such puzzles solved and some of my questions answered. In some ways one could regard life as being deciduous: we slowly shed abilities like leaves, and end as atoms in the ground, and then are recycled.

> I am a thousand winds that blow.
> I am the diamond glints on snow.
> I am the sunlight on ripening corn.
> I am the gentle autumn's rain.
>
> Anon

- and that is a faith, a belief, call it what you will, which makes no demands on credulity and draws no sceptre or sword.

The next sign, one of the standard black and white council type, noted 'Easter Muirhead 200 yards. Tethyknowe 1.5 miles.' This was not really extravagant for Muirhead Stables was the largest such establishment I've ever seen, a whole row of stables and a vast shed for the horses to perform under cover. No visitors this 'gruey' day. In several long stable blocks I saw rows of horses' heads hanging over the half doors. I hoped they appreciated someone's choice of pop music going full blast. Wheely bins bore the logo of Perth and Kinross. The fields beyond had horses under blankets (I could have done with one too). Visibility was never more than about two hundred yards. A grass road seemed to run alongside the tarmac, at one stage was overgrown by gorse and birch trees. The road kept alongside for one, then a second, right road bend, before angling off by a birch fringe to a wood named

Lambhill Moss. The reason for this still escapes me. Notes were pinned here and there asking people to contact a number if they chanced on any escaped Highland cows. The fields were much more mushy and very wet. Hoof marks were filled with water. I often heard the squelching of cows feet before seeing them through the mist. This zigzagging wee road was another 40 mph Walkers and Cyclists Friendly one. A female walker came up behind me to make me start. We then had to squeeze into the verge to let a horse box and several cars pass. Almost every farm or big house seemed to be in the horse business, Rivendale Boarding Kennels excepted. Cars were few and far between. Cyclists were a regular feature. I always heard them coming. Cyclists talk.

A Forestry Commission sign, Barnhill, had me study the map. A track to and beyond this farm led to the foot of Cult Hill, which the Border circles, and which I wanted to climb, but if this approach didn't work I'd have a long retreat. The road would give surer access, from greater height, and maybe the mist would clear by then. The walk throughout had enjoyed a 'mellow fruitfulness' but this was a harsher reality at autumn's end. The haws were blackened and the brambles, according to an old saying, revealed 'the devil had pissed on them'.

Howfold farm noted that it supplied milk to Sainsbury's. There was a huge barn and along the top there was a line of starlings. There must have been over a hundred. The garden had swings and a big tree house. A magpie flew off, just a recognised silhouette. There was a robin. Several of them worked the hedgerows during the day, low down, while above, there were occasional blue or great tits. A quarrel of rooks occupied a row of dead trees. Geese flew over often. Was there a greater urgency in their calling this bitter day? A flurry of long tailed tits blew through. There was always birds to see. No pheasants, surprisingly. A big new house was another equine establishment, with horsebox and *manége*, the square protected by a planting of Scots pine. A nice touch: the entrance wall had one of the grey capstones replaced by a chunky white quartz one. All the usual trees had been noted: oaks, still holding their leaves, plenty ash (dire reports on ash being killed off in England), and, the glory of birch and beech, a last swanking of colours. There was a mist-modified din now and then from the Knockhill Racing Circuit. Saturday. Cairnfold Farm was also 'Dollar Equestrian' which had me remembering teenage years when I helped at the Lower Mains stables in Dollar, mucking out, combing, and taking children out, all for the odd chance of riding a pony back afterwards. I did have one thrilling gallop through Glenquey from Glendevon back to Dollar. I was brought back to the present as a runner came round a bend and, perforce, did a neat swerve not to crash into me: an enviable lean type, in his prime. Damn it! I'm not old; just suffering a deficiency of youth syndrome.

I was never a runner; too sturdy of build (when a reporter once mentioned 'trim Mr Brown' my friends hooted). I'm built for the long haul, like all the Munros in a single self-propelled walk. I was thinking about this when the runner passed because a couple of days before I heard the news that a Skye lad, Donnie Campbell, had just set a new record for the Munros in one go: 31 days, 23 hours, 2 minutes. I took 112 days! That is not comparing like with like: I was taking the challenge slowly and carefully simply to prove the thing was possible. (Previous attempts had failed, largely because bodies ran out of 'go'.) The idea of creating any record was never in mind. But competition soon developed; and running the Munros has simply become another branch of mountain activities. Some Munroists are a bit snooty about such doings but why not? Each to his own – and admire the other. Perhaps I have more empathy, because for doing them in a single walk, for records or for fun, there are common elements, which can be called logistics. I covered innumerable maps with a line to link all the Munros and finally had to put my choice to the test. I began in Mull and ended on Ben Hope and that has been a common factor, but every record breaker has fine-tuned the route and all the practical matters like eating and sleeping. Donnie's record is astonishing: he was beating the 39 days plus by Stephen Pyke, set in 2010. [In June 2023 the record was shaved to 27 days by a lass Jamie Aarons, starting on Mull and finishing on Klibreck.] Any of these super athletes would have run my route from Kincardine to Newburgh in one day! They were fliers, I'm a plodder.

After idling along past the Tethyknowe road end, my route turned to aim more determinedly uphill, and into Fife, though I only realised that when the next wheely bins seen bore the Fife logo. The brae quickly silenced two more cyclists who overtook me. The next farm was Busses, which I thought might be 'bushes' as that's how a Fifer might say it, but the derivation seems to be the plural of an old word for cattle houses. The name first appears in 1562. Heather and blaeberry were appearing on the road banks and there was one bright campion in flower; with a many-headed knapweed earlier, they were really the last, lingering, verge flowers for 2020. My walk had been spread over the good days of October but now November had slipped in. With the height gained, the fields held sheep rather than cows. At the next junction I managed to climb a gate and find a suitable stone to sit on to have my picnic, and time out. Suddenly a silvery sun was shining through overhead and, momentarily there was a bloom of blue sky. The promised clearance?

There was a rustle in the hedgerow behind me but I was too lazy to investigate. Whatever was there was welcome. Later I kicked myself for not looking: there might have been a weasel or slow worm or hedgehog, even a snake. I like adders. We saw them at schoolboy camps at Ballater and became quite blasé about their proximity. They were there first after all.

I saw adders regularly up on the moors above Deeside and on one occasion showed a whole squirming newborn family to a passing lady – who turned out to be Princess Margaret – but then, the royals' presence on Deeside was equally unremarkable. Once a year a camp team went to Balmoral Castle to play cricket against a scratch team of residents and visitors, royals or not, all organised by the Duke of Edinburgh. I wasn't a good enough cricketer to make the team ever, but do recall one happy occasion when President Eisenhower was at Balmoral. There was an

American boy, Philips, on camp who would be thrilled to meet his President so he went along as scorer for the game, and did indeed meet Ike. I bet he still talks about it.

A Morrison's van clattered past. Knockhill cars started to roar again. Time to move: the last mile up to the A823. Off left I could see scattered trees through the mist then, on the last gentle straight I was looking to a skyline of hills, spread above the mist. Momentarily, the whole sky above was blue, and the temperature shot down to near zero, before mist gobbled up everything once more. In that brief gap a thrum of starlings careered past. The mist had made the hills look enormous and, when I turned north along the A823 Crieff road, a muckle pyramid soared out of the mist with what looked a mighty range beyond. I had to persuade myself this was Cult Hill, which was only three fields off. The symmetry, crowned with a trig point, was startling too. My spirits soared at the sight and also with the realisation that the Void of Fife had been crossed, and crossed happily, despite being forced to walk tarmac for most of the crazy Border line. Cult Hill beckoned. I must have been at 200 metres elevation on the road and the summit was 264 metres or just a couple of hundred feet in old style climbing. I'd been fascinated by how Fife's border had lassoed the hill into its territory so just had to climb it. Not so cheering, turning along the A823 looked the best continuation thereafter. Cars frighten me far more than hills.

A gap with a gate led to a wall line that aimed straight up the hill so, even with the mist rolling in again, navigation would be simple. So it was, but I was ambushed by something else. I'd not taken more than a dozen steps along the wreck of wall before my feet were soaked. (But they had to be, surely, to be the walk's normal?) The hill was very green and all round the base the map marked springs, but the rough pasture symbols I'd taken as a good sign. I left a trail in the wet grass and often the surface was water-logged (not always visible!). I'd been spoiled, obviously, by Fife's manicured farmlands. The wall was decayed as was a fence on one side and, where there were favourite places for sheep to cross, they were marked by a convergence of muddy tracks and wool caught on the barbed wire. The first field ended in a slight dip and I sat on a stone awhile hoping the mist would clear but there were only tantalising glimpses of that beckoning trig. Concern about access to the next field vanished: another wrecked wall. On both sides of the ongoing upward wall there were big flocks of sheep grazing. Oddly, this wall had been rebuilt and had a good fence on both sides. Running off left was a row of dead trees, all very spooky in the conditions. A murder of crows ghosted through, and I *heard* oystercatchers. The second field was even wetter underfoot. A last fence and final steepening, passing a hollow (old quarry?), and a crest led up to the trig. I gave the trig a thoughtful pat and, as if in gratitude, the mist rolled away. Wow, oh wow! 'Only a hill; but all of life to me,/ Up there, between the sunset and the sea' (G. W. Young).

I stood with the sea of cloud all round and seemingly contained by huge hills, the Ochils wall to the north, Saline and Cleish Hills to south and east. The turning arms of wind generators above Glendevon were slicing through the woolly surface. That was all I had time to take in for, at once, I was re-enveloped in cloud. I sat, back to the trig, till dangerously chilled and then had to scamper down as I'd come, to warm up again. (There's a prehistoric fort on a bump NW of the summit, but all evidence was grassed over.) I had better views on subsequent visits when the ground was perfectly dry and my wellies a joke. Being such sheep pasturage, visitors would be best to avoid the lambing season. But do choose a good day in summer or autumn to enjoy the exceptional 360-degree panoramic views.

The cloud was disappointing as I'd climbed Cult Hill for a variety of reasons, including studying the Border and the topography generally. The Cleish Hills run east-west, most of their forested sprawl in Kinross, but with a north west Fife prong leading out to Cult Hill, and a larger prong rounding south for Knock Hill and Saline Hill. The westering Border runs along the southern foot of the Cleish hills as far as the last hill (Wether Hill, 335m) then heads straight over and down to the north, to then encircle Cult Hill to Tethyknowe, all quite illogical. But at least Fife had possessed Cult Hill.

I'd also climbed Cult Hill because the hill looks across to the parts of the Ochils and Devon Valley where I passed my schooldays from the age of ten. Before that I was wandering far afield: Sri Lanka, Japan, Malaya, South Africa.[4] Not three miles

4 I was born in Ceylon (Sri Lanka) and my young brother was born in Japan, thanks to father's postings, then we were chased out of Malaya to Southa Africa for a coupe of happy years. From mother's letters home, my own memories, and father's account of his ship bombed and sunk, I told the family saga in the book *East of West, West of East* (Sandstone, 2018)

west is the hamlet of Blairingone (There and gone!), which shows something of the weird effects of Border designations; the postcode is FK (Falkirk), the address Clackmannanshire, and council tax is paid to Perth and Kinross.

The county boundaries of my schooldays were quite different. I could walk five minutes from home in Dollar to be in Perthshire, now a chunk more of Ochils and River Devon has become Clackmannanshire, the wee county, taking a bite out of Perthshire, the very area I explored most. Explore I did. I could go where I pleased. I knew every farm (just over there the one where we went tatty howkin), every burn (there, the one where I learned to guddle trout) and every hill, glen and moss back to the natural bounds of the Ochils–held River Devon. This river rises far in the western Ochils, not four miles north of Menstrie and enters the River Forth not two miles south of the same Hillfoots town yet the river is circa 23 miles long.

The Devon flows west-east through the heart of the Ochils as far as the breach of Glen Eagles – Glen Devon. (Three reservoirs have appeared on the river in my lifetime.) It exits on to the plains between conical Seamab Hill and bulkier Lendrick Hill to the Yetts o' Muckhart (*yetts* is gates), then wends on to Crook of Devon where the river makes an elbow turn to flow west all along the abruptfront of the Ochils. The word Crook is apt for, at one time, the river flowed cross country, on to enter Loch Leven. The term is river capture; the Devon wore back, glaciers altered landform (or whatever the cause), so the river makes this about turn, and soon reaches Rumbling Bridge, another apposite name.

This is one of Scotland's great secret places. The river has carved out a narrow gorge like no other (well, the Black Rock of Novar perhaps) through which the water churns mightily. Because the water never stopped turning, even on Sundays, folk bestowed the name, the Devil's Mill. The gorge continues to conclude with a spouting of the Cauldron Linn. The gorge is bridged, hence the name, bridged long ago and then a second, wider bridge was added – on top of the first: bridge over bridge. The next bridge down-river is Vicar's Bridge, named after one Thomas Forest, a kindly man who was burnt at the stake because he read the Bible in English, an early Reformation martyr. We had a favourite swimming pool there but the river changed shape and the pool has gone, perhaps because the old bridge was replaced. The older river name was Dovan or Dowan but had been anglicised by C18, for a poem of Robert Burns refers to 'the clear winding Devon'.

When home again I had a careful look at the OS maps and, yes, there is no impediment to the Devon having carried on across the flat plains to reach Loch Leven (whose level was higher at the time). The watershed separating flow to Loch Leven and the flow westwards is extraordinary. The Gairney Water which enters the SW corner of Loch Leven has its upper water almost at Rumbling Bridge, while much of the drainage lying north of Cult Hill joins the River Devon (confusingly by another Gairney burn). And a northerly-running watershed marks the headwaters of the River Eden.

Recently a new allure has been added to the area: a couple of miles east from Dollar, lies the exquisite Japanese Gardens, first made in Edwardian times, and recently restored, a unique Scottish feature. Book yourself a visit.

No wonder I sat on top of Cult Hill till near frozen. Some day I'd return, but wearing wellies. I was still mulling over these thoughts when back on the A823. Home all my adult life has been on the Fife coast, the coast of the River Forth. Being born in Colombo made me no less a Fifer, nor was my young brother Japanese, nor my mother Siamese, by the chance of their birthplaces. Big brother and father were born in Dunfermline where there was quite a family clan. The earliest Browns traced were C18 shoemakers in Dysart. Looking at the names of my eight great grandparents however shows a remarkable range of geographical markers, from East Lothian to Ayrshire, and northern Argyll, Perthshire and Caithness. There's some sad history behind such movements to Lowland Scotland and, another diaspora of my grandfather/father's generation, saw his brothers and sisters and their children scattered worldwide. Scotland's greatest export has always been her people.

Back to the A823 I didn't see much option but to walk along the road to near the Knockhill entrance and head off from Outh Bridge to reach Park Hill. Reading of my experiences doing this the next day might suggest wiser alternatives, but subsequent visits, and talking to Tilhill forester and Outh Hill shepherd confirmed there are no short cuts. To be fair, I'd later wander the same route in an

August heatwave with boringly little bother; the November finishing off the Border walk next day was much more memorable.

Being Saturday there were mainly cars racing past on the A823, and no HGVs. The A823 can be a busy road with a ration of manic drivers. Walk it at your own peril! I passed houses called Sunnyside and Broombush, Hillside, Inkerman, North Letham and Outh. The slopes to my left were forested but, to the right, the view was one I always admired motoring this grand highway: a bowl of upper valley that drained as the Black Devon.

On the right as I walked a blackbird was playing that annoying game of flitting ahead whenever I drew near and I wanted a closer look at this one; something wasn't quite right. When the bird was forced to cross the road into the trees I saw there were primary feathers which were off-white in colour but quite distinctive. Years ago I did see a mostly-white bird and recently, in a magazine, a photo of a pure white (leucitic) swallow which looked very strange. This white appearing can happen to creatures as well (a photo recently of a white squirrel) and flowers. As a youngster I spent hours not finding out what a small flower was that I'd found. The flower looked just like a milkwort but milkworts were blue – then one book mentioned that, occasionally, they can be white. A weasel, obviously failing to look right, left and right again, torpedoed out onto the road, then, seeing me, did a back flip and shot back into the wall; how one usually sees weasels.

Rising out of the mist Knock Hill and undulating Saline Hill still looked exaggeratingly impressive. Sheep came streaming up a field to me as I reached North Letham Bridge where a forest track (Tilhill) heads up towards Scaur Hill of the Cleish range (a fine viewpoint), one route I'd considered for easting but, with others, rejected. The surest start looked like being Outh Bridge. A couple were stretching tape between posts for an electric fence and hailed me, "Not seen anyone walking this road in years". My thought (and probably theirs) was that only daft gowks walked A roads, so I explained what I was up to (which no doubt confirmed their doubts as to my sanity).

When the forest ended, and before North Lethans, there is a gate. Taking this, I thought, might skirt the forest edge, and lead to good-looking Park Hill. Tested, this proved no option. One first has to continue along the road - and this led me into 'a mess in a moss' as you'll read.

Cars on trailers were being towed off from Knockhill. With only an hour of daylight remaining the sun blinked out sporadically. Geese flew over in endless noisy arrowheads. I rang a Dunfermline taxi number and sat at Outh Bridge to empty my water bottle and scoff my remaining cheese with Ben Gunn enthusiasm. The fog lasted the whole run down, and dusk at sea level came slowly and surly.

Over sixty years ago I wrote about a more cheerful 'May Day on the Cleish Hills'.

> Alone,
> With the spiralled song of the lark;
> Alone,
> With the winds of the wild grey hill –
> When the day is fired in the kiln for night
> And eyes alive with the sights of the height.
> Alone,
> With the peewit's skeery screaming,
> Alone,
> Where the heart of the land lies still –
> When the air grows cool and the heart glows bright,
> When the step goes tired and the thoughts go light.

Chapter Three

PRESENT FORESTS, PAST MINING

Two men eyed the wood:
An artist, dreaming; a merchant
Making estimates.

The Cleish Hills

THE NAME, OUTH Muir, on the bounds of the old Dunfermlineshire, intrigued me. 'Outh' also appears in Outh Hill, Outh Park, Outh Plantation and Outh Bridge. The word tasted of antiquity and so research was to prove; a charter showed King William (the Lion) granting the King's forest of Outh to his illegitimate son, Robert of London, who then passed the lands to Dunfermline Abbey. The name is on Bleau and Roy maps and may come from the Gaelic for breast, from the rounded shape of Outh Hill. So Outh was where I would set off from to traverse the Cleish Hills, taking a more logical line I may say than the Border did.

One temptation, soon dismissed, had been to drop down to the other side of the hills after Cult Hill and then up very steep ground (on the Border) to Wether Hill to try and keep through the forested high ground. But a big loss of height just to climb up again didn't appeal. At Outh Bridge I was actually higher than Cult Hill. I also chose the start there hoping to explore this wet desert a bit. One sink hole was mentioned, near Outh Bridge, and streams had breaks in their flow which might be interesting. One thing was sure: this day would be made wearing my mini-wellies. The forecast was for a mainly cloudy day 'with some sunny intervals' and, heading off by taxi from Dunfermline, I noticed the ex-firestation's tower had been caught in a noose of sunlight.

This was in fact a second setting off from home for the Cleish Hills, so I'd better confess to what happened then. I had hoped to use the one dry day forecast in a miserable spell of wind and wet, thus I was up at 05.30 for an 06.20 bus to Dunfermline, arriving 07.30. A taxi on up to Outh Bridge, at Knockhill, would make a good early start to win through by hills, lochs and forests, to Kelty. I'd set off from the coast in rain but, by Dunfermline, the sky was clearing. Somehow though, in the words of Gaston Rebuffat, 'the human animal was not happy'. There was a bullying wind, which would be a fighting wind (plus clouds with clout) on the heights and the ground right from the start would be super-wet. 'Glaury'. Grim going. I wanted better for what was the most serious day of the Border ploy – the only one for which I had someone alerted as to my doings and ready to dial 999 if I hadn't phoned in by dark. I'm very sensitive to hill moods, theirs or mine; I just did not want to proceed. The hills have an endless reserve of surprises to catch us out.

I went in to the Dunfermline Tesco for tea and a bacon roll and sat at the window watching the sky steadily clearing. Magpies were chasing each other through the top of the trees in the glen below, trees which were having their leaves torn away by the wind. Here was a day to walk low-level and west-east (wind behind), and one not to be wasted either, so I took a bus to Kelty and walked the south shore of Loch Ore and explored the Country Park which I once knew well, and had a pleasant day instead of a 'what might have been' day. No regret. Every day is a gift. More: the Cleish Hills stayed hidden under a 'solid continent of scowling cloud' (RLS) and even Loch Ore was having a winnowing wind. My hunch had been right.

Thus I was setting off again by taxi from Dunfermline, at a more humane hour, which soon proved frustrating after the sunblink start. Every one of the traffic lights on the way jumped to red on nearing it, there were other reds to allow streams of Queen Anne High School pupils to cross, there were reds for road works, and a ration of constipated HGVs to tail. One of those days. The driver had to phone in and say he'd not be able to do his school run. He was remarkably phlegmatic but then that was his world. He was a bit nonplussed when I stopped the car "in the middle of nowhere". My world.

A farm track, deeply churned up by tractor use, headed off to heaven knows where, following above a surprisingly deep trench of the Nettly Burn. A group of big black heifers stood to their knees in black goo; one beast moved off, fighting, foot by foot, freeing the mud with repulsive sooking sounds. I took to the grassy flank on a rising traverse which took me through the area marking 'shafts (dis)' and 'shake hole', which proved disappointing. Looking back, the Knock's masts were being wrapped in mist, then, with some height gained, I had my first wide view over Outh Muir. Whatever the moor's interests, I was not heading into what was, patently, one great invidious marshland. So? I'd have to round the 310m hill I was on (White Hills on the map) to outflank or climb 324m Outh Hill and hope the watershed from there to Park Hill would 'go'. No sooner was this decided on than I was enveloped in mist and all visibility vanished. Far from being miffed at this mutinous act, I thought "Good. This will be fun". So it was, of its kind.

I continued contouring, by the feel of the land, to drop down a steep bank, onto what would be the saddle to Outh Hill. I set a compass course due north to flank along Outh Hill. The ground was all marsh, moss, rushes and pools, tussock and runnels, needing every step to be watched. Then I came to a slinky burn too wide to loup, especially with very shaky banks. The struggle on up-burn was sometimes desperate and I won through largely going from one clump of rushes to another with mini mishaps in plenty. My whole world was watery, and I felt was just waiting for a misplaced foot to gobble me up.

That must have been near the start of the Nettly Burn which is shown rising on the Outh saddle and heads off eastwards, bifurcating, to then add other burns and cross the whole basin to its own crook at the far forest edge, and then head back west to Outh Bridge. The mist moved and gave glimpses of this marvellously unforgiving landscape. I made my tortuous way over to slightly steepening ground, so began contouring round on marginally firmer going. A brief, high up clearance, showed a huge hill rising from the mist. This fake was Park Hill, 339m, recognisable from its map contourings, and satisfyingly, appearing where it should have been. This was fun! I kept to my dedicated contouring till I decided the time had come to chance crossing to Park Hill and, at that stage, the mist happily rolled away for good. The hills sometimes take pity on their devotees.

I'd picked up a 'trod', and this I could see led across the quagmire to the SW foot of the prow of Park Hill, the last bit of trod looking like a possible wheeled track. The trod was water-filled and at times spread into odorous black morass which had to be circumnavigated. Would stream or streams prove impassible? The map shows three wiggly burns merging as one, then this vanishing, reappearing, vanishing, reappearing, before, in the heart of the wasteland joining the Nettly. I was very relieved to come on one, two, three duckboard-like bridges lying on the rushy streams. They were rather decayed and I tiptoed across on the edges where there was a supporting beam underneath. There were traces of an ATV track which went off eastward at the foot of the hill. I sat on some rocks, relieved that I'd won through so – relatively – unscathed. Mist still trailed round the Knockhill masts. There was a bird soaring high overhead, on the verge of human eyes' capabilities, so I lay back to watch, imagining what the bird's view would be, my mind free to spiral along with it. Had I at once trotted out a speculative name, I would have pigeon-holed a fact and diminished an experience.

I was quite sorry the mist had chosen to move on. I find tricky navigation one of the most exhilarating of mountain experiences, utterly absorbing. This was something I enjoyed teaching too – seeing the joy on the face of a youngster who had his objective Munro cairn loom up just where expected after an hour of careful navigation through an intricate landscape in cloud.

I always made navigation important to my school lads. "Map to compass to ground" was something of a mantra. A Silva compass dangling round a boy's neck was like a badge of office. But basic feel for landscape can be even simpler. Most lads had their first experience of the wilds staying in the school's hut/bothy in the huge Black Wood of Rannoch, where they ranged quite happily, knowing how to find home if they were mislaid. All water ran down to Loch Rannoch. The bothy was on the lochside road. QED. There was a case in the Welsh Carneddau at that time when a school group, caught in mist, pitched tents and waited for the clouds to lift. They were found 36 hours later, and praised for what they had done. When one boy said he'd have given them a kick up the posterior (not his word), I asked why. "They only needed to follow the burn to come to somewhere." (A farm less than two miles away.) Sit and wait for cloud to lift?

Refreshed, I followed a trod, at a maximum possible angle, up and across the steep west face of Park Hill. Sheep had worn out sheltering hollows into the hillside to confirm I was on a sheep track. Ewes obviously don't have our fear of steep slopes. There was a flatter area and a wrinkle or two up to the summit. A single stone, overgrown by grass, marked the spot. Looking back over the moor's boglands my line chosen was clear and I felt a real satisfaction over hitting a route so well. 'A backward glance can oft lift the heart' (Dante). Park Hill, too, was the only major Cleish Hills summit I had never stood on previously.

West, to Wether Hill, their summits lay much lower. These hills look a bit like a lumpy serving of pudding over which a custard of trees has been poured. There isn't really a summit ridge. Volcanic activity must have been lively at the birth of the Cleish Hills. An old guide called the hills here 'pleasantly unconventional'. The plain down north has something of a moat along its length: the Bow Burn which becomes the Gairney Water. The odd inclusion of Cult Hill in Fife looks as if the Border is following the watershed. From Cleish Hills to Ochils is a thoroughly confused landscape. From there the Cleish Hills appear simply as a tree-covered stretch of upland. What Park Hill gave me, I decided, was the most complete view of the Ochils, from the far steepening in the west to the slow softening in the east. But I would repeat that thought on the Georgeton Hills and then Dumglow, and had to give Dumglow the palm. Norman's Law was quite clear from Dumglow. The Highland Hills were too faint to interest. Looking down to work out my onward route I watched a buzzard lazily working along the face of the hills. No doubt about that identity.

I dropped down to the col with Black Hill and skirted up to join a wall which was the forest boundary – and Fife's. Kinross may possess Dumglow but Fife has Park Hill. Oddly, there was no trod along by the wall and I had an awkward crossing. When I gently touched the wire along the top with a dried grass, the grass jumped. But the voltage was low when I inadvertently touched the wire myself. I wended on to head up the marked cone of the Georgeton Hills, 349m. Over by the trees a deer was grazing. A roe. I crouched to watch, sure the beast would not scent me but, after a while her head came up, she dithered and then treaded slowly off out of sight. I had noted two people passing along at a lower level from Dumglow so maybe the roe had heard or scented them. From Park Hill I had picked out four people by the trig point on

Dumglow. The Black Loch, set in the roots of the hill, was the colour of pewter and the sky was beaten tin in tone. White dots on the Black Loch were gulls in a lazy flotilla.

I watched the two lads use a gap along from where I'd crossed the wall and head along the ridge. I kept looking but they never appeared on the slope of Park Hill so I worked out (well, speculated) that they would skirt the forest edge to the A823, while the other two I'd seen on top returned to their car to go round and meet them. I came on a wetted puffball, and without thinking gave a wee squeeze to see if it was in working order. Yes; out puffed the spores. (I mention more about puffballs during the Pitmedden Forest day.) One well-attested use of puffballs in the past was to apply the inner skin of the cup to a wound to stop the bleeding.

An essential part of walking is the not walking, the break punctuating the walking, the resting restoration of feet and feelings. A broken stone dyke made a good place for my main pause of the day: a piece on cheese, peanut butter and tomato. And a jammy one. I was to enjoy the break for several reasons. Heather was growing profusely and in its depths I saw something shiny. I found a button, one cut from mother-of-pearl shell, old fashioned, so could have lain there for decades. I pocketed the trophy to add to the inherited button-jar in my sewing basket. That ages me. No buttons were thrown out when I was a boy. If a garment was being disposed of, any buttons would be cut off. "You never know when you might need one" – and I sometimes do, today, and the jar never fails to produce a matching button to the one lost.

The stones of the wall were covered in a variety of lichens and I passed some time looking at them under my magnifier, enjoying their exquisite beauty. What just looks a grey, smudged circle on a rock can be revealed as amazing artwork, detail denied to the casual eye. One here was a mass of thin, dark spikes, each tipped with a particle of light, water perhaps; another had a pale, smoother surface covered in geometrical polka dots; in the heather were bright orangy-red blobs of *Cladonia* which, under the magnifier, looked like sumptuous, exotic fruits.

When I noticed mist drifting in round Park Hill I moved on. I was chilling anyway with a breeze which was more teasing than annoying. From Park Hill I had been gladdened to see the western prow of Dumglow split by a wide grassy gully, for the hill has a prehistoric fort on top with just a defensive wall on the long, easy-angled eastern slope, the rest being defended by cliffs. Gap there may have been but the slope was contour lines-squashed-together steep, so would be no easy option for attackers, or for me. Lungs and calves were given work to do and I was happy at times to use the fence running up the slope as a handrail. Breathless I flung me on the windy summit, to misquote Rupert Brooke.

I steadied binoculars on the trig point of my airy mountain to survey the world. Yes, Dumglow had the best views of the day, but '... fleecy clouds were wandering in thick flocks along the mountains, shepherded by the slow unwilling wind' – that's Shelley, but his words held good. The Ochils were catching the advancing clouds. Glasgow would be wet. Time to press on, leave *the fort of strife*; of which little is visible.

A very clear path led off which I presumed would go down the forest boundary to the Black Loch and along to edge Loch Glow. A bit of path did continue down the forest edge but a much larger one turned into the forest. As I'd crossed a substantial stile with waymarking arrows on it I assumed things had improved over the years since I'd been there last. Certainly Blairadam Forest had many marked routes. So I took the path into the forest.

Just before reaching the stile I'd a very different brief raptor incident: the passing of a one-speed sparrowhawk. No mistaking that flight, in that sort of place. The first I'd ever seen, as a boy, was by a wood edge near Loch Droma, an encounter not likely to be forgotten. I put up a pipit and the rising bird was grabbed a few inches in front of my face by a sparrowhawk racing past.

The forest was of big conifers, forming regimented verticles in a sterile gloom, the ground churned up into a wide avenue of black mud. Cycle tyre ruts were ribbons of water. One pleasant surprise was seeing the trees edging the break were festooned with the greenest moss I've ever come on, a decorative delight. The path was not on the maps, but led out to many acres of cleared trees, which looked something like a front line landscape in World War One. A forestry road (on the maps) came in from the north, the arms of a signpost rather oddly indicating 'Kirkhill Common 1.25, Dumglow .5, Loch Glow .75'.

A very wet, mossy, unconstructed path led on along the felled area, with trees on the right, to a stile onto open ground but failed to provide any directions at that point. I sat on a stump for a break and was rewarded by a close view of a kestrel, which trembled overhead all the time I was there. Ten minutes later I spotted a second kestrel, once I had walked through a gap in the Inneans, a group of hills before me, hills enjoying 'a contorted smallness' (RLS), the group lined roughly south-north. I thought the name sounded just how a Fifer might say 'onions' but the derivation is from *inneoin*, an anvil. Two hills were facing me, a third, to the north, lies overwhelmed in forest and a last bump is Dummiefarline (locally, the Dummie). A huge skein of programmed geese went over on their irresistible journey, bullying each other on noisily. I wandered about a bit but there was no further route indication and something of a plethora of path choices, the most clear heading on through between the Inneans. This I took, though I'm sure the 'Loch Glow .75' sign I'd passed meant I should simply descend the forest edge path now to the loch, the dam, and the stony track out to the over-the-hills Cleish road. But this I did not want to do. My Fife Border is never that simple.

Below Dumglow, the Fife Border dropped down to the Black Loch and then along the north side of Loch Glow to its dam. A forestry road comes in to the dam from the minor road over to Cleish, but I knew felling work had shut that natural way on for me. From the dam however a channel, the Lead, headed NE on the edge of the forest (and as the Border) to reach the Cleish road too, at Lurg Bridge, whence the flow continued as a burn, heading down by Chapman's Grave and the west end of the Nevingston Craigs – waterfalls – to join the Gairney Water and eventually enter Loch Leven. Where Loch Glow's original outflow ran I have no idea.

I'd long been curious about the Lead so, with the track out closed, I might follow the Lead as an alternative. But could I do so by continuing from where I was, keeping high, pass the Inneans and drop down directly rather than a dog leg by the dam? I relish these sort of puzzles, that lead to decisions, that lead to whatever befalls. It is a truism that people who 'never go alone' remain incomplete, for only by going alone are decisions forced on one and a true feel for the mountains obtained.

A good path did tempt me on through the Inneans and I was rewarded by a classic view, a composition that would have made any artists purr, for the slopes of the hills, left and right, framed the view while a dominant Benarty filled the centre, with a touch of distant Loch Leven, left, and far Largo Law, right. John Constable would have smiled. I know I did.

When the ground fell away before me all smiles stopped. The ground fell away steeply to two lochans sited half way over to the Lead (Lurg Loch, Dow Loch) but the ground looked all too like Outh Muir and the same warning symbols graced the map.

A careful survey however picked out faint trods and heathery areas so I took the chance and descended. The ground certainly was wet; I squelched in water at every step, staggered tussock to tussock, and only made progress step by step, each having to be sure before another was chanced. Tiring work. About fifty yards from the Lead a toe became trapped under a tussock as I stepped forward and, as if shot, I was brought to my knees. The day may have ended with dry feet (for once) but the front of my trousers was soaked.

The Lead proved a substantial cut, but there was no path alongside, so I worked through quaking rushes to reach the wee road. (The only sign of the road had been the white diamonds of the passing place signs.) Barbed wire guarded the road, but I was saved by a self-seeded sturdy spruce growing in the corner above where the Lead burbled off under the road. I was glad no cars passed, though I'm sure a pair of ravens sporting overhead were having a laugh at my expense. I fought up the antagonistic tree to pass feet, one by one, safely over the barbed wire and then lower myself slowly. I had to cross; I'd thrown over my rucksack, binocs and beanie hat. The Border turns right to run along the road for several hundred yards before angling left to enter Blairadam Forest proper. Was I going to be able to do likewise?

Blairadam Forest

God may have made birdsong and trees;
man created the cage and the axe.
Anon.

Yes I would be able to follow the track. There wasn't a 'No Entry' sign due to felling, as had happened when I'd walked through the forest once before on a more southerly line. Instead there was a rather reassuring sign, Path to Maryburgh 2.25 (a hamlet just north of Keltybridge). Border and I set off then, the Border soon breaking off to follow the Pieries Burn downwards to become the

Kelty Burn, an unusually long stretch where the Border follows a natural feature.

A couple of drives went off to invisible Bonny Brae and Millwood and a rather grand new house loomed ahead, just before the track was enveloped by forestry. A buzzard was posted on top of a skeleton tree, but then launched out gracefully on broad wings. An older name for the bird was *gled* which meant glider. After two lazy spirals it dropped out of sight behind the trees. I could see a notice ahead by the verge of the track and wondered if the words would be, 'No Entry' after all. I had to reach Kelty, that's where I'd find bus routes, so I almost laughed to read the notice, which was apologising to visitors that the surface was such a mess, because of necessary upgrading.

The track had been doubled in size, with margins brutally hacked back, and the surface bore a resemblance to sticky toffee pudding. Thanks to the grand old duke and wellingtons! Incidentally, one can still sometimes hear or read people saying wellies should not be worn on the hills and usually giving fatuous reasons like, for instance, they've no decent tread. Most wellies are worn by farmers, builders and the like who are on far nastier ground than walkers, and most wellies have, in reality, deeper, better treads. I was completely taken by wee wellies when climbing in Norway many years ago; everyone seemed to be wearing them, in a land where the rocks were rockier, the bogs boggier, and the vegetation fiercer (and the midges were bigger too – they were mosquitos!) At the end of this day, while sitting in the bus, I could wiggle toes in dry socks – and watch the steam rising from my knees.

The road was 'gey slaistery' and bootprints wandered about where walkers had avoided the worst of the evil. One mark showed where someone had gone for a skite (slide) and, judging by hand prints, landed on his bottom. Over the day I must have saved an hour by wearing my wee wellies. I met an unhappy-looking woman picking her way along and received a wan smile. Her big, very big, very hairy dog had a sort of plimsoll line on his flank: fur above, a mess below. I grabbed his collar when he ran up to say hello, voicing "Nice doggie! Aren't you having fun? No! Don't you dare jump up on me."

The wood to my left (north) was Cowden Wood which tried to encircle Cowden Hill but the north flank is just too steep for commercial forestry. After another straight bit of tacky track I came to a cross-roads. Up left I could see a communications mast, straight on no doubt led to Maryburgh, while, right, lay my route, still a gluey road being pushed through for future developments. I could hear the saws down in the working area.

> I hate the sound of a saw,
> Raw, like some monster beast
> Tearing prey. I turned back
> In my local wood yesterday,
> Not wanting an encounter.
> Today, Sunday, the wood is still
> But my walk was distraught
> For I had come on a victim
> And counted rings. Two hundred.
> Yet the saw took two minutes
> To rend the years and gralloch

Life out of those centuries.
Clear-felling they call it, but I
Am not clear at all. Did they
Have to cut so deep, in tree,
In me?

In the words of Pooh, it was 'time for a little something,' but where to rest? In the end I sat in the brash-filled ditch to use the slope of the bank, which was heaped with the slashings of everything within a certain distance, the cuts still vivid, like wounds. I could smell the hurt. The weather was growing grumpy to match my mood. I was tiring obviously. But, from now, the walking was all downhill. That prospect cheered me up, as did having to concentrate on the map, as any wrong turn would have demanded careful extricating. At last I came on an expected complex road crossing, audible felling off right with a warning sign on the road, off left an unreformed road which wiggled all over the place and returned to the same spot, but, ahead, a kindly red gritty footpath which led down to a Pieries Burn Bridge and then a larger bridge with added metal barriers within the stone parapets. This crossed the main stream, what was the Kelty Burn, draining East Bow Muir, tributaries starting near the wee Cleish road. The map shows a lattice of blue lines which indicate drainage channels. A direct random A to B traverse of this mature forest would be a nightmare. I found a yellow marker post then twisted down to the cheery burn, one almost large enough to call a river. The sun came out as if to apologise for its poor attendance all day. I met a lass with two of the friendliest, silky-coated golden retrievers, who were introduced as Toffee and Fudge.

The burn was flowing 'darksome brown' with stones capped with white froth, lively enough to make pleasant music. A huge, solid block of bricks puzzled but, with a similar one across the river as well, probably was a bridge abutment, maybe for a mining line. I found out later that that was correct and this was once the Hundred Foot Bridge. A stream joined in from the right, had its boulders the colour of tablet and came out from under a wide, small arch of a bridge – except there was no road over it or at all visible. A puzzle. Upstream, the water was rustier-coloured, a mining connection no doubt. The glen path criss-crossed the river several times and, with the burn as the Border, I wondered who maintained it, Fife or Kinross. The trees became older, grander. There was one area of sturdy beech, the colours vibrant in the westering sun, a sun which striped the ground beyond with gold between tall conifers. This was quite the most benign hour of Border following so far on my pilgrimage, but I love grown-up forests.

Some concrete slabs and hummocks among the trees was where the small Blairenbathie mine once stood. It started in 1895 but was badly affected by geological faults and intrusions and closed in the 1925 slump, only to open again after WW2, then closed for good in 1962.

I had my last break of the day, sitting on my waterproof on a bank – the contentment of just sitting -- to demolish my regular walk-ending boost of one or two or four dark chocolate peppermint squares. A dunnock was mousing among the ferns, a woodpecker was a faint presence far off, the trees overhead I'd swear were swaying to the breeze in waltz time. Then a dog rushed past, a hyperactive springer spaniel, a species with no slow in its gearing, guzzling a world of scents, high on those hidden sensations. I didn't exist.

A mossy twig caught my eye and I took out my magnifier to look into the delicacy of the minute exotic colour and mathematical complexity. A beetle was working through what, to it, was a contrary jungle. Where did it think it was going? Why? Eventually I placed the twig down, no longer seeing it as just a mossy twig, there was another world lying hidden there. I was surrounded by worlds within worlds. I, too, am really a very tiny creature.

A twinge in my, as yet, unrestored hip had me up to proceed, but there was a scurrying. I'd bothered a red squirrel. I was puzzled for a moment as this fellow was unusually dark in colour. The squirrel raced up a pine in front of me, rushed out and back along some sweeping branches, then stopped on one directly overhead where there was a great shaking and waving of tail. I took the hint, walked on, no doubt a grin on my face. A glance back saw it racing far up the trunk. The squirrel too has a world within worlds.

A junction had signs for a route to Kelty using a footbridge over the M90 but would divert well off the Border line. I did explore that way later when the autumn colours had covered the ground instead of the trees. Just ten minutes along was a big car-park where all the wood's colour-coded trails began. A tarred road runs in from the South Lodge on the B914, west of Kelty. There was also a Fife Pilgrim Way sticker at the car-parking centre. That route had come wandering up from Dunfermline to follow the drive in, then to head, as I will, for Kelty by the Border, but then veers off into the Lochore Meadows Country Park, rounding the north side of Loch Ore, and heading east, passes south of the Fife Energy Park with its deep water holes. My Border continuation, though not indicated as such, was for Kelty by Keltybridge, still heading downstream. North of here was a rather special forest tract – where Blairadam forest had its inception.

What was Blaircrambeth estate was bought by the architect William Adam (1684-1748) and he began the centuries of tree planting – 'for usefulness and profit with enjoyment and ornament'. There was only a solitary tree on the land he bought. (He was also investing in coal mining.) He built Blairadam House as a family home. Son, Robert (1728-1792), became the most famous architect of his day, which is recalled by the Adam style, Adam period etc. William Adam's most celebrated works were Hopetoun House and Duff House, and the famous 'Wade' bridge at Aberfeldy. His building firm in Kirkcaldy was the largest in the country. Robert was born in Kirkcaldy (as was his friend Adam Smith). Culzean Castle was Robert's most notable Scottish mansion.

Sir Walter Scott was a frequent visitor to Blairadam, the guest of William Adam, grandson of the above William. A group of nine formed the Blairadam Club who met for relaxation and social stimulus at chosen weekends. On the Saturday they would ride to some historic site or sight, Sunday they attended Creich Church, and dispersed after a Monday morning outing, as Adam had legal obligations in Edinburgh. Scott used to talk to an old servant who had an endless fund of stories. The group became suspicious when local stories and places seemed to be clearly described in the Waverley Novels (then with the author unknown) so, when what looked like the Kiery Crags, above the Kelty burn, appeared in *The Abbot,* he was challenged directly during one outing and the secret of authorship was out.

Burn-burble gave way to motorway hubbub. Looking up I could see that the Welcome to Perth and Kinross sign had the usual addition of Kinross displayed. Long live wee Kinross, second only to Clackmannanshire – when we had counties. A farm, redolent with the smell of bovines, lay beyond the M90 tunnel. A last neat bridge took me over to the Kinross side. The area had an oldie-world feel, the houses firmly rooted, one telling a story in its name 'Phoenix Mill'. At the tarmac I turned right, crossed back into Fife, and reached the north end of Kelty's Main Street. First left, Black Road, would be my continuation of chasing the Border, not that that was mentioned, the sign was for Lochore Country Park, three miles away. Before reaching the park however the Border, illogical as ever, shoots up onto, and along, Benarty.

Walking into Kelty, at one place I had to step off the pavement as a hedge had been long neglected, as had the once-orderly garden it imprisoned. All was Darwinian fight: shrubs sumo-wrestling each other, once neatly-spaced flowers having a brawl, lawn commandeered by dandelions. Oddly, as I wandered on I began thinking of a contrast to this where, in Morocco, neglect had a very different result.

A road runs below the length of the Atlas Mountains, a great south road, separating mountains and desert; in places it also separates two tectonic plates so one can stand on top of a ragged ridge running to horizons, and, down slope, in one direction is Africa of the Sahara, in the other down slope is Europe of so many green dreams. Africa is still inching into Europe. One day, far ahead, Africa will have gobbled up the sea separating the continents. The road is often majestic in its loneliness, running through a landscape largely stripped bare of possible prosperity, left to the winds and the sun. Where more natural to plant a portion of the 60 million trees to mark the king's 60th birthday? You can see the hollows running alongside the road for many miles where, indeed, the trees were planted, watered – and then left; to perish because provision was never made for any follow-up or maintenance. Scottish negligence is seldom so stark, but too often people only know and accept the present as the satisfactory norm, as what has always been, so the degradation of our world goes unperceived.

In retrospect, Kelty seemed to have more heart than the sprawl of one-time mining villages on the other side of Loch Ore and I'll describe why next. To complete this day I naturally stopped off to find a café for the almost statutory coffee (and brownie), and still managed to be home on the gloaming. The long day had proved that the 'setting out with cheerful expectation had a returning with pleasurable satisfaction', doubly so as today was in reality the last section, last day, to be slotted in to the Border ploy. My Border had, so to speak, two endings: here and Newburgh.

Kelty and King Coal

Kelty has three eye-catching monuments to the mining days that were the town's reason for being. The first was only a few minutes along Main Street at the northern end, a small engine inscribed Wee Chief AC 527. This is a replica of a working engine and was made by apprentices at Babcock Rosyth in 2011 ('supervised by shipwright Dougie Young'). There was information on the Aitken Pit, which operated from about 1899 to 1963, and the Blairenbathie. The Aitken had a workforce of about 1250, so think of the total numbers involved with a dozen collieries hereabouts and round Loch Ore; think of the families struggling to make do, in the end seeing the industry die. Mining was hard and dangerous work, but it was work and, with some security, made real communities.

This area was once called Whitegates, where a line came from the Blairenbathie and then out towards the Aitken. Kelty was for almost a century a large marshalling yard (hence the replica engine) with lines coming in from four directions: SW, from Lillieleaf (near Townhill); SE, from Aitken pit and Lumphinnans; W, through Blairadam forest from Blairenbathie; east through Lochore meadows, from Kinglassie. The Mary and Kinglassie single line ran through Loch Ore on a raised bank to reach Kelty (the line of islands today). The Mary pit, beyond Loch Ore, was linked 1.5 miles, underground, with Kelty's Aitken mine – and was used in one emergency. In 1942 miners marooned in the Glencraig also escaped via the Mary. Two escape routes were made mandatory early on, hence most collieries having two shafts.

At the side of the open space fronting the Community Centre on Main Street is a statue of a miner, dressed as he would be, ready to enter the cage and descend to work, a figure completely true to life and rather moving. The sculptor was Fife resident David Annand. What men they were: unassumingly brave, loyal, tough, kind, who never had the respect, or the pay they deserved. 'There is always more misery among the lower classes than there is humanity in the higher' noted Victor Hugo. There's a circle on the ground naming the area's collieries: Blairenbathie, Lassodie, Aitken, Mary, Benarty, Peeweep, Lindsay. In the last named, in December 1957, nine miners were killed in an underground explosion.

The worst ever Fife disaster was at the Valleyfield Pit near Culross in 1939, when 35 miners were killed and 26 injured. The mine was notorious for fire damp (methane) to the extent the gas was being piped into the public gas supply. A spark could be fatal – and was. Yet work continued in those conditions.

While heading for the third monument look out for another one-time feature in mining districts. Down at the traffic lights, facing the 1896 parish church is the Kings pub. This was originally the No 1 Goth, opened in 1900, based on the Swedish (Gothenburg) scheme of providing better premises and services than the normal run of pubs which were often just drinking dens. Profits went into the community to provide facilities for recreation, street lighting, libraries and the like. The beer was also less likely to be adulterated. There is another 'Red Goth', facing the Miners' Institute in Lochore, but a Goth in Kinglassie has also dropped the name, and the Crosshill one has gone, as has No 2 Goth in Kelty, across the road from No 1 Goth. The Crosshill pub was not strictly a Goth, but modelled on the system. Following the 1927 strike Crosshill Cricket Club was established.

There certainly was a great deal of drunken behaviour. Kelty had five pubs then, and booze was easily obtained elsewhere too, but there also existed the embedded Scottish trait of seeking self-improvement. The Library was well-used and included a reading room, recreation room and billiard room, while many miners were keen sportsmen or outdoor enthusiasts. The Kings (No 1 Goth) is on the corner of Station Road and this is followed to the third commemorate site, at the junction with the B996, the Great North Road. Here we see a model designed by Jim Douglas, of a pithead winding gear in red and white and a bogie for carrying coal painted black, and marked Fife Coal Company Wagon 2783. Dates of collieries are given, for Benarty, Aitken, Lindsay, Peeweep (Peewit). What a pity the OS maps don't mark and name them, but then, for most there is nothing to see now. This, for instance, was where the Lindsay Colliery sprawled.

Lassodie was a series of licenced mines situated north of Loch Fitty, a couple of miles south of Kelty. Accommodation was built, there was a school, a Free Kirk, two Co-ops, and a pub. In the early C20 there were 200 houses for 1400 people, with four working pits but there was endless geological trouble and flooding and in

1931 they were closed and the miners and their families forced to move. The place was simply abandoned and by the end of WW2 all signs of the past had disappeared. In the 1990s the area would be gobbled up by the vast St Ninian's Opencast workings, that site still visible from the M90. Marked 'Meml' on the OS map, by the B012 just before it crosses the M90 heading north, is a poignant war memorial giving the names of twenty one men who died in World War One, from this place that no longer exists.

The Lindsay had employed 800 miners and was connected to the Aitken, NE of the Lindsay, half way to Loch Ore. The Aitken employed over 1000 miners at the peak in 1956 and had its own powerstation, once the largest in the country. Both would close in the cruel 1960's. The Peewit or Peeweep lay about 1000 metres NE of the Aitken, and operated 1896-1966, becoming a surface mine in 1946. The name comes from the vest or singlet the miners wore. (I'd assumed the name was from the bird!) After WW1 a fire in the Lindsay engine house spread but somehow the cage was saved. Miners below had to use the underground connection to the Aitken to escape.

Glenrothes, the town, was originally envisaged as a modern, attractive showpiece to match the super Glenrothes Mine. This opened in 1957 with the hope of producing '5000 tons a day for a hundred years'. From the start the mine struggled with a fractious geology and flooding and, when the estimated cost of £1.6 million passed the £20 million mark, closure was inevitable; in 1962.

The Pilgrim Way wends through Glenrothes by the pleasant Riverside Park, then heads east to the last of the mining towns,

Kinglassie, with St Andrews, the journey's end, still some way off. Ian Bradley's book, *The Fife Pilgrim Way* 2019, has an interesting chapter about mining, particularly in this region where the route becomes something of a mining trail. One book he quotes was by an American journalist, and social reformer, Kellogg Durland, who passed four months living and working with miners in Kelty in 1902. He must have been a tough cookie. Some other interesting figures are worth noting before going on. A Corporal David Hunter, a miner from Kingseat colliery near Dunfermline, won the VC in WW1. In 1920 he posed for Joseph Epstein for a piece to represent all the Scottish VC winners. The bust stands in the Imperial War Museum. Kelty miner, Robert Stewart, beat an American, Newell Bank, to become the World Draughts Champion in 1922, a title he held until he retired, unbeaten, in 1937. Stewart only lost one game in 5000, would play several boards simultaneously and even play blindfolded.

Waiting for the bus I was entertained by two pied wagtails. They were searching round the war memorial and pavement, dib-dibbing so rapidly – at who knows what? They worked along to the feet of a couple of young adults sitting on a bench with their chip suppers. The pair were obviously intrigued by these birds, which behave so like mechanical toys. I half-expected the birds to be thrown a chip. When one of the birds went pedalling off in a rush, legs a blur, as only a wagtail can, the couple laughed at the sight. That was good.

I make no apology for dwelling on this area's mining past. To children today mining may just be history but, to some, mining is 'not history, but hurt'. When I was a teacher, I was in a mining area and I shared that hurt of the final collapse of mining, which included the deaths of miners in an accident, men whose kids I taught. The resulting fall in population would see the school itself made redundant. Like earlier salt-panning on the coast, mining is slipping from memory to become elusive history, leaving hardly a trace.

But to end on a more cheery note. Kelty stars in a song which captured the period brilliantly: 'The Kelty Clippie'. This was written by John Watt and released in 1986. John died in 2011 (his definitive album, *Heroes* Neon Productions, is still available). John had been involved with Jack Beck, and others, in starting up *The Howff* in Dunfermline in 1961 – in the cellar of a chemist's shop which had been a wartime air raid shelter. *The Howff* became one of Scotland's most famous Folk Club venues where everyone, but everyone, performed.

Over my coffee in the cheery café Essen I asked some lassies if they knew 'The Kelty Clippie'. They didn't (What's a clippie?) but an old dear demolishing a cake with her cuppa heard and said she remembered the song fine – and even made a gallant attempt on the first stanza, which act as a chorus. I was told the Kelty Clippie could be seen in the library across the road, so of course had to meet her – the very image of the song, *People's Friend* on lap and fag in hand. There was also a cabinet with a collection of miners' lamps and finely-detailed mining models.

THE KELTY CLIPPIE

Oh, she's just a Kelty Clippie,
She'll no' tak' nae advice;
It's "Ach drap deid, awa' bile yer heid,
Ah'll punch yer ticket twice."
Her faither's just a waister,
Her mither's on the game,
She's just a Kelty clippie
But I love her just the same.

Frae the pyramids up in Kelty
Tae the mansions in Glencraig,
We've trod the bings together
In mony's the blyth stravaig:
Watched the moonlight over Crosshill,
Trod Buckhaven's golden sand,
And mony's the happy oor we've spent
In Lochgelly's Happy Land.

Well I met her on the 'eight fifteen'
That night o'romantic bliss.
I says "Hey Mag pit doon yer bag
And gie's a wee bit kiss."
Well she didnae tak' that kindly,
No she didnae like ma chaff,
And being a contrary kind o' lass
She says "Come oan – get aff."

Noo she hisnae got nae culture,
Ach she drives me roon' the bend,
She sits every nicht in an old arm chair
Readin' the 'People's Friend.'
Her lapels is fu' o' badges
Frae Butlins doon at Ayr,
And she gangs tae the Bingo every nicht
Wi' the curlers still in her hair.

But things is a wee bit better noo,
Ah've gone and bocht the ring;

I won it frae Jim at the Pitch and Toss
Last nicht at the Lindsay Bing.
Wi' her wee black hat and her ticket machine
She did ma heart ensnare,
She's the Lily o' Lumphinnans,
She's ma bonnie Maggie Blair.

On the bus from Kelty a group of teenagers were energetically talking about Hearts football team. I don't follow soccer closely, but there was something strange in what I overheard, and why should Kelty lads be so keen on an Edinburgh team?? Weeks later, looking at a newspaper's sports pages over a coffee I did note there was a *Kelty Hearts* team and on the verge of promotion to League Two. No wonder the bus lads were excited. (They have now been promoted to League One!)

Homing to Burntisland via Kirkcaldy was a more attractive route than going via Dunfermline, besides it was a route less taken and attractively rural. Either way a No 7 Dumf–Leven service passed two minutes walk away from where I live – or four minutes if I included the 56 steps to my flat. The steps are a bit of a curiosity. The first flight, of twelve, rises to a half-landing, the first of three which in Victorian times led to add-on toilets, then turns to go up seven steps to flats 3 and 4. The next set of steps, ten and nine, led to flats 5 and 6, and the last, ten and eight, to flats 7 and 8. So one side has twelve, ten, ten steps (total 32), the other seven, nine, eight steps (total 24) yet all the flats are on a level. What is going on?

Guests find it hard to sit down in my eyrie of a flat. They just stand at the window to look out over the Links, railway, sands and sea to the cone of North Berwick Law and the hump of Bass Rock. Last thing at night I always check on the lights on Inchkeith and on Fidra (which masks the Bass light), which so marks the end of journeyings. I am a happy man for whom being out and doing is good, but very satisfying too is the returning home from the doing. Cleish Hills, the forest, to Kelty was by far the longest walking day, so I was home with the stars blooming like flowers opening, and the comfort of the looming lights out at sea.

Clackmannanshire Bridge (AS)

Tulliallan Kirkyard: The Tree-Feller Stone (HB)

Roadside Notice in the Void of Fife (AS)

Emu at Solsgirth (AS)

In the Cleish Hills (Dummifarline) (HB)

Hamish in the Blairadam Forest (AS)

The Kelty Mining Monuments

Wee Chief (loco) (AS)

Wheel and Wagon (AS)

Miner (AS)

The Keltie Clippie (RD)

Loch Ore Visitors Centre and the
Mary Pit Winding Tower (HB)

On Benarty Hills with Distant Ochils (HB)

The Lomonds Across Loch Leven ~ The Bishop (HB)

Paragliders on the Lomonds (HB)

West Lomond (HB)

Carlin Maggie on Bishop Hill (HB)

Bunnet Stane (Shutterstock)

Harvesting in the Howe of Fife (RD)

Hamish on the Path to Bunnet Stane (HB)

To the Lomonds from along the high road (Balcanquhal) (RD)

Balvaird Castle (RD)

Lochmill Loch (HB)

River Tay from Macduff's Cross (RD)

Macduff's Cross (RD)

In Newburgh High Street (AS)

Old Lintel in Newburgh High Street (AS)

The distillery from the Abbey Ruins, Newburgh (AS)

The Arch (AS)
Marking the end, or the start of
The Fife Coastal Path

Chapter Four

FIFE'S HEIGHTS

*If you climb up high
You will have the sunrise first
And be warmed, longest.*

Benarty

I HAVE A saying for a hill day that is near perfect: a day of glory given. Today was one: the travel clicked, the logistics performed, the weather was brilliant and the rewards sang. I didn't even mind the alarm going off at 05.30.

Back when the French Revolution was worrying everyone in Britain, a retired, eccentric politician, Sir Michael Malcolm of Lochore, wrote lines which resonated today. 'Happy the man who belongs to no party,/ But sits in his ain hoose and looks at Benarty'. Benarty is 356m (1168ft), well-defined and offers splendid all round viewing, the only busy hill on my route.

Kirkcaldy is known as the lang toon but Kelty's main thoroughfare deserves the name just as much. The first good mark for the day was that the bus went the whole length of Main Street to the north end, where the Border came out of Blairadam Forest. I simply crossed to walk down Black Road and was soon out in countryside, walking beside a den to a junction with the B996, marked on the map as Great North Road. Today that duty falls to the M90 which squeezes Kelty on the west. Near the skirts of Benarty is Parenwell, a bridge that was built simply as a memorial. There is no stream below the span. The oddity was erected by

William Adam to commemorate Mary Queen of Scots fleeing this way and avoiding a planned abduction, after her escape from Loch Leven Castle. Her day's ride ended at Niddry Castle near Broxburn. At least her equestrian abilities cannot be doubted! A roadless, riverless bridge fascinated me as a boy. Scott had Adam inscribe the story on panels attached to the bridge which have faded today.

Five minutes along the B996 I came to the Border, a standard Perth and Kinross sign with the additional Kinross in place. A few minutes later I swung right onto a small road that leads into the Lochore Meadows Country Park. I crossed back into Fife, at the site of the one-time Benarty surface mine, which closed in 1959. The coal was taken to the washery at Kelty's Aitken colliery. Soon after I turned onto a drive to Blair Mill. A path led on by what the OS named The Den, which was just that, a wooded dell, such a common feature where Fife hills gentle down into lowlands. Most such were of no use for cultivation so were left for nature's arboreal 'improving'. (I rather cringe at many descriptions of 'improvements'. They are often the opposite. The Germans have a word for this: *verschlimmbesserung*.)

On leaving The Den at the entrance drive of Benarty House, five minutes west along the quiet road that heads from the M90 to Ballingry led me back to the Boundary line which ran straight up Benarty and then along above the northern scarp; certainly the most pleasant length of Border to be so easily walked. A brisk north wind indicated cattle ahead. They had churned up the wee burn that edged the line awhile, the fence giving in to an invasion of whin, more usually called gorse and sometimes furze. Three steepening fields led to Benarty's crest and a mighty explosion of a view. Looking south, as I climbed, had been steadily bringing in Fife's comfortable, lived-in landscape, and many particular landmarks into view, but I'll save repetitions and render a summit glut once there. I nearly trod on a chilled bumble bee which was struggling in some heather so I picked it up and breathed some warmth into it, saw it revive, tremble, and take off like a helicopter. Nearing the crest a glider was circling constantly, each approach announced by a wuthering of wind on its wings. At the crest I almost ducked. Three gliders, almost wing tip to wing tip, were heading straight at me. Did I imagine a laugh when they swept over? Up on the left is a prehistoric fort of unusual size and constructed with huge stones, the walls circling out from a northern natural defence of cliff.

There was a surprisingly steep-sided gap in the ridge as I went on, the crest now all heather, to reach the stark trig point. I first stepped to the rim. Below me a buzzard was being harassed by two crows. One of the lagoons beside Loch Leven was almost invisible below a covering of geese. They had been flying in from all directions as I plodded up, yet the strong wind carried away their din. Earlier, I'd felt it strange to watch the frantic M90 traffic yet hear nothing. That I had a birds' eye view of Loch Leven hardly needs saying. I had a good look at the Lomonds on the other side: thence ran Fife's Border.

Loch Leven is most famous for two things: the trout fishing (Defoe noted, 'the finest trouts in the world') and the well-authenticated story of Mary Queen of Scots escaping from Castle Island, where she had been imprisoned. Before the lowering of the loch the castle more or less *was* the island. In 1335 it was one of a few strongholds holding out for hapless David II when the English overran Scotland. A rather hopeless attempt was made to dam the outflow to raise the loch level and so force a surrender, but they failed as the scheme was beyond C14 technology. Odd, that 400 years later, with somewhat improved technology, the level of the loch was lowered – and Castle Island doubled in size. The castle was a royal possession till awarded to the Douglas family in 1390. When Mary was held there, after her surrender at Carberry, it was held by Sir Robert Douglas, a relative of the Earl of Morton and step-father of Regent Moray. Yet Queen Mary escaped largely through the aid of a young page, Willie Douglas, who filched the keys and rowed her ashore. Much good it did her: Mary escaped on the second of May, was defeated at the Battle of Langside on the thirteenth and crossed into England on the seventeenth. She had, in full, the Stewarts' natural talent for disasters. Defoe visited both Castle Island and St Serf's on his tour round Fife and Kinross.

The Benarty spelling appears on older references as Ben Airty, Balnarthy, Wynarty, Binnarty and Bannerty. The derivation might be from Arthur, the legendary figure. There are other Arthurian Scottish sites: for example the Cobbler (hill) is Ben Arthur to the OS. The Ochils (an anagram of Slioch) look quite grand from Benarty. I was asked if one peak was Schiehallion. The peak was Ben Vorlich which, with its flat-topped twin Stuc a' Chroin, lay in mirror image to how so often seen by motorists descending Glen

Ogle. The Highland hills to the north were hazed, but binoculars picked out endless intrusive wind farms on their margin. I left my daysack at the fence to wander over to the trig. The panorama spread from Bass Rock to Tinto, the Pentlands in oceanic roll across the south. So much to pick out: the three Forth bridges (on the way up just the apexes of the new bridge showed but the mighty railway bridge was catching the sun and looked as if burnished), the near bulk of Moss Moran, the distant spread of Grangemouth, the huge crane at Rosyth with sorry cruise ships in the dockyard and the masts atop Knock Hill in the nearer Cleish Hills, so recently walked. Loch Ore lay right below, whose rebirth I had witnessed after Ballingry, Lochore, Crosshill, Lochgelly, the heart of Fife's mining industry, had collapsed, and the land (and the people) had been left desolate, the landscape scarred with bings, floodings, railway remains and abandoned buildings. I find it a wonder now that out of such dereliction came the Loch Ore Meadows Country Park. Praise where praise is due, for Fife Council.

Walking back to my rucksack something dived down into the void beyond – a peregrine, stooping after some careless victim. A couple who came and chatted had seen one earlier. The sun shone hotly and I had to take off a layer of clothes, yet a few steps away a snell blast was shooting up the crags (and thereby leaving this nook tranquil). A cyclist appeared at the trig, standing haloed in the sun. Next, a couple arrived, the man with a baby on board.

Several people stood over me to chat as I sat demolishing a hard-boiled egg, a slice of Cheddar, and a tomato, eaten with pepper oatcakes. I was asked other questions about what was in view; many were clearly being thrilled, and made curious, by novel experiences of comprehensive hill panoramas. Lawers – Schiehallion – Beinn a' Ghlo – Cairngorms might have been glimpsed, but were too hazy to pick out. Global warming cropped up in conversation and I thought of the Ochils (so bold in the view, with their rolling green quilting and abrupt frontage) where I had an inkling of the topic long before they began to be given capital letters. The Burn of Sorrow rises in Maddy Moss which was, when I was a boy, just that, a moss/marsh over which one picked a careful route. Today the 'moss' has become 'rough pasture' as the ground has dried out.

Over a score of people came and went during the time I had my snack, the busiest time and place of the whole Border following. Why so busy? But, of course, this was a very sunny Saturday. Benarty presented a great escape from daily life below. Up here all were kings. I could feel the joy. Heading off again I met two couples, each man with baby on back. After that I met nobody; back to the bliss of solitude. Walking is free and gives a freedom impossible in most pastime activities. I think covid-19 has seen many discover this simple truth. 'Thousands of tired, nerve-shaken, over-civilised people are beginning to find that going to the mountains is going home; that the wilderness is a necessity' (John Muir). The natural world is beautiful, restorative and necessary, yes is vulnerable, from our actions. But sometimes, as with covid, it gave shocking reminders of our own vulnerability.

A clear path ran along the crest, steep drop on the left, heather moor on the right, gliders overhead. There is a pleasant circular walk up to Vane Hill from the popular Vane Farm (now renamed Loch Leven RSPB) which nestles down by the loch. RSPB bought Vane Farm in 1967 and have created an important freshwater site for wintering and/or breeding wildfowl, with an ever-busy Visitor Centre.

The path I was on swung south but, at a lower level, a ridge continued eastwards with bright green fields and with what interested me on its crest, the prehistoric fort of Dunmore. My path came to a gate into woodland, Benarty Wood, but I turned down on a small path, which dropped to a well-made path which came, I now know, from the Vane, but was leading me off course, south, as hedged by a meshed fence with barbed wire on top, impossible to cross. I was a bit 'scunnered', but just when it looked as if I'd have to miss the fort, the top strand of fence became ordinary wire: crossable! A few sheep moved off as I followed field edges again, one ewe with a damaged back leg that had her barely able to walk, yet whenever the beasts stopped, she was nibbling like the rest. I wonder if the shepherd knew he had a casualty.

And mentioning shepherds, I came across something about their doings on the summit of Benarty. In ancient times they organised games on top, the summit being both level and sufficiently large an area for what was quite a shindig. The current word might be 'rave'. Men from all over Lochoreshire, and elsewhere, gathered. Wives, daughters and lovers came up. I suspect the games of strength, and rowdy football battles would soon lead to scenes that would have needed the pen of Rabbie Burns to describe. This went on for several days, everyone bivouacking at night and presumably ended when refreshments ran out.

Dunmore gave a wind-battering scramble and seemed more crag than anything man-made but the summit felt right and, descending the other less-steep side, there were remnant walls of huge stones. The Border keeps along this ridge, slightly down on the left, before descending to Ballingry's NE corner and then making a sortie towards the Energy Park. I had a good look for the morrow, and for today's more immediate concern; how to enter Ballingry, for the whole lower hill slope was lined with houses. One small area of trees on the map looked hopeful and, after a devious descent through slopes taken over by gorse, I found a gate by the wood. Q.E.D. For a change, every possible check to progress in the day had proved non-existent, the sun and the wind and piling clouds had been exhilarating; a day of glory given.

The ending of the Benarty day was blessed as well. Entering, and then exiting, what seemed like a football ground, (no stands but enclosed) I came out to a road which was the required bus route, and there beheld a NISA shop – with a coffee machine. I walked along to a bus stance and was looking at timetables when a lady informed me, "Bus coming, sonny. Is it your number?" Yes. And not every day do I get addressed as 'sonny'.

Ballingry to Leslie

When we see the land as a community to which we belong, we may begin to use it with love and respect.

Aldo Leopold.

Ballingry's parish kirk was one of the few old buildings lost among the many clumpings of housing schemes. The bell is rung by an outside chain and is inscribed 'Malcolm of Lochore. 1658'. Sir Walter Scott's eldest son married a Jane Jobson (of Lochore) and Scott often visited. As a result the church has a mention in *The Abbot*, his romantic tale of Mary Queen of Scots imprisoned in Loch Leven Castle. Burns warning could apply very well to Scott, about 'a chiel amang you takin notes/ And faith, he'll prent it' [print it]. Ballingry (pro. Bingry) comes from the Gaelic *baile* (town) and *garadh* (flowers/garden). Nestling under the hill, the town could well have been a flowery wee place; being known as Bonny Bingry. But that would change: the population in 1841 was 436, in 1931 the population was 10,353. Defoe came this way on spying out the country, but only noticed Lochore Ore, Loch Fitty and Loch Gelly. Coal was yet to be crowned. He did mention the Adam plantations at Blairadam.

Just across the road from where I caught the bus, from and back to Ballingry, I came on a neat memorial garden: in memory of all the men and women and children who worked in the Fife coalfields. In Fife alone mining would account for 2,317 fatalities, never mind the thousands of others who died before their time through damage to limbs and lungs. There's a stone saved from a Miners Welfare Institute (1926) and all through the succession of towns, Ballingry, Lochore, Crosshill, Lochgelly, there were halls and centres created for the welfare of miners. One walks through those towns with ghosts. A display board in the garden mentions the two local collieries, the Mary and the Glencraig. The latter was opened in 1895 and had two shafts. The first sod for the Mary was cut in 1902 by the wife of the manager of the Fife Coal Company and a second shaft sunk in 1923. The Mary's winding gear was made by the German firm Krupps, the first such pithead frame in Scotland to be made of reinforced concrete. When the coal industry was nationalised in 1947 the Mary employed 600 miners and the Glencraig 910. The Glencraig was linked underground to the Mary and also southwards to the Nellie just outside Lochgelly. Unfortunately there was serious rat infestation, due to ponies (and their feed) used underground.

Walking round the garden I spotted another mournful notice, one pointing out 18 December 2015 as the day the last UK coal came up from a deep mine (earmarked for a museum) and named the last miner, one John Marshall of Kellingley Colliery in the north of England. The garden is symbolic in another way. Fife is green and pleasant, so what happened to all the coal bings and the dirt and squalor left behind when the industry died? Fife was tidied up, the greening hard-earned. Loch Ore had been drained in 1790 to create land for agriculture, but it could flood in bad weather and there was subsidence as well. When mining expanded the redd was just dumped more or less on site, bings almost overwhelming homes. The pollution must have been grim. There are reminders of this past. The Mary colliery pithead frame is still there (beside the golf course), with a bright green and red

NCB (National Coal Board) railway engine standing alongside. An interpretative board records 78 names of the miners who lost their lives in the Mary colliery in the years 1903 – 1965. A replica pit winding wheel stands at the park's main entrance, these the only signs of a once teeming industry. Also by the entrance is the decayed ruin of Lochore (Inchgall) Castle which once was situated on an island, which looks improbable, but simply shows the scale of the landscape alterations. Walks round Loch Ore are, rightly, popular.

Whether following sporting activities on the water, or on the land, or just walking the dog, or letting the kids loose on the extensive play area, or sitting on a bench, the park has been a boon for the rather undistinguished towns around it. The most striking building along the B920 linking the towns is the Lochore Miners Social Club with a somewhat skewbald mix of harling and red sandstone and topped by a disproportionately small clock tower. The Red Goth faces it. Bradley suggests the Goths could be revamped as hostelries for pilgrims. Good idea. My stravaiging must have been some sort of pilgrimage. An unkind friend suggested the walk was more penance.

An important part of Fife's plan to clean up all the bings and dereliction left from the mining years was the building of a power station at the mouth of the River Leven, which was to be fuelled by the waste material from all over Fife. A lifespan of twenty years or so was given to gobble up all the bings. Basically, the slurry was blasted through finer and finer meshes till the consistency of talcum powder and when that was fired there was a very powerful blast. I was always amused when passing in icy winter to see a large congregation of swans on the sea at the works. They had discovered an outflow of *warm* water. Once the notable environmental task was complete (and remember this was half a century ago, before there was much environmental conscious-ness) there was some thought given to keeping the power station operational.

In those days all Edinburgh's drains (some medieval still functioning perfectly well) ended up at a treatment plant in Leith. There was a certain amount of recycling and various grades of sands and gravels were sorted out. I recall someone there shaking his head at the metals pile. "How on earth does someone manage to dump a push bike into a sewer?" The remaining sludge was loaded onto a ship, the *Gardyloo*, [5] and taken out into the North Sea and dumped. The captain, Ronnie Leask, was a friend of mine and I sailed twice with the *Gardyloo*, once to near the Bell Rock and, next voyage, beyond the Bass Rock. A free day aboard was a council P.R. exercise and was perfectly pleasant: breakfast, lunch and, if late back, supper all provided. As can be imagined the most eager passengers were ornithologists. E.U. Regulations were making themselves felt and dumping at sea was to stop; might, just might, this rather different slurry be taken

5 This was an imaginative name for the council to come up with for its waste-disposal vessel. In Edinburgh, late C17 – early C19, the Old Town's High Street was the city's main residential area. Sanitisation was hardly known. Rubbish was just dumped in the streets and liquids were thrown from upper windows with the cry, 'Gardyloo!', from the French 'garde a' l'eau': 'watch out for water' – which was putting it euphemistically.

to Levenmouth and blasted through to keep the power station going? Alas, no. The site was mothballed and then demolished. But as one wag said to me, "Pity. I'd like to have imagined every time someone flushed a loo in Edinburgh the lights went up in Fife."

The early part of the C20, pre-World War One, was the main period of mining activities. At its peak in 1957 Fife had something like 24,000 miners, producing 10 million tons of coal each year. The forecast was that the coal would never run out. And coal did not run out (I wonder if we might return to coal sometime in the future), the industry simply could not compete with cheaper imported coal and the general shift to oil. Economics, the smiler, and the killer. Once begun there was almost a domino effect in mines closing so rapidly in the sorry Sixties, the result being high unemployment, social deprivation, and a degraded environment. If the rural has repossessed the mining sites, the towns themselves still bear quiet psychological scars. Many miners had come in from Ayrshire and Lanarkshire, but Fife seemed to have avoided the religious bigotry elsewhere, but Fife miners were highly political – with good cause.

If conditions in the mines have always been tough and dangerous, they were far worse in previous centuries when miners were simply serfs (no other word fits) If that was done away with in 1775, we still had children as young as eight employed and women *carried* the coal to the surface or were forced to push waggons up inclines. Hours were long, safety measures non-existent and wages allowing only subsistence living. Pithead baths only became available after nationalisation in

1947 for instance. Fife coalfields were the first in Scotland to achieve an eight hour day – in 1870. Because of the endless struggle for decent wages and conditions, strikes were not uncommon and local councils often had a Communist representative and one famous MP, Willie Gallacher, who probably needed an interpreter at Westminster.

How quickly vast industries, employing tens of thousands of people can come and go. In 1832 Lochgelly, for instance, was principally a weaving village, and weaving was Fife's largest industry, but in 1836 mineral rights were granted and Lochgelly became something of a boom town; Ballingry may have been an ancient parish, but was nothing more than a hamlet before King Coal arrived. These towns just happened, rows of cottages added indiscriminately as new shafts were sunk, and even after the mining ceased, conglomerates of housing estates mushroomed almost randomly. There was no centre. Shoppers headed off by tram to Cowdenbeath or Dunfermline. Sadly, with the mines vanishing, so did many of its traditional sports and pastimes. I can recall pigeon racing, 'the dogs', and seeing quoiting (pro. kite-ing) in East Wemyss. It would be the same here. Pipe bands were active, cycling had its followers and football was played rather than watched. A century earlier there was even llicit cockfighting. I can also recall seeing bings on fire, smoke rolling across these mini-mountainscapes. My pupils still collected sea coal – coal returned by the tides from redd that was dumped into the sea. A village at Buckhaven was completely buried under the redd and bings by Lochore, forced people to be rehoused before their cottages were overwhelmed.

As a teacher in the sixties I had one other Lochgelly connection: the tawse, a two-tongued leather strap which was applied to the palms of miscreants. I may say I received more beltings as a pupil than I ever applied as a teacher. I didn't need the Lochgelly, the tawse, the strap, call it what you will, and in 1983 this barbarism was phased out.

Starting off again on my walk I could see likely problems when continuing from Ballingry. Soon after leaving the town the Border line went down and round the vast Fife Environmental Energy Park (Westfield), a circling of which did not look viable on foot. Oddly invisible from where I stood were the dual artificial 'lochs' marking the one-time open cast mine workings.

Westfield I knew all through the years, from being annoyed when a small road I used to drive was closed off in the early sixties and on to the site's demise in 1987. From Benarty the waters had looked grey and uninviting, alongside the industrial complex and ever-present pylons. When Westfield was in full production I was flown over the site and saw the work in a unique fashion for, from ground level, nothing was visible (carefully made so) and one had no idea of the reality. The walls were terraced down, down, to a pit where minute tracks drove on a maze of levels. A grey pond occupied the lowest point. The rim was a mile and a half round. I was informed that 'when coal extraction is done, the hole can be filled in again and the land reclaimed for agriculture'. Filled in with what though? Twenty million tonnes had been extracted. I was looking down into the depths of a super volcano, I thought. Filling proved to be with water, 800 feet or more deep, which may be one reason there is no recreational use. Kinninmonth, on the north rim, had to be rebuilt, as the farm was in danger of sliding into the maw. Work had started in 1955 and the site was exhausted twenty five years later. Now a wind farm sprawls on the site.

The Border line, having tangled with Westfield, then shot back over a crest to drop down to the Leven cut. This was then followed for three miles down to Auchmuir Bridge, beyond which I knew there was a riverside right-of-way to Leslie. Could you walk this artificial waterside line? And which side, if it was possible? There was no path shown on my maps. I'd be a bit put-out to descend to the New Gullet bridge, find no paths, and then have to toil back uphill. And in that contourless flat bottom fence lines were *blue* (or black and blue), indicating almost every field was edged with a ditch. How would they be crossed? Though I'd face some road walking, I opted out, wisely as it proved, when I was informed later in the day that there wasn't any passage along the cut for pedestrians.

The cut was made in 1826-1832 (cost £36,000) which lowered the level of Loch Leven, to reclaim 1,400 acres of land and give better control of the water flow, vital for the many bleachfields and mills of all kinds along the River Leven. 85% of Loch Leven is only fifteen feet deep and the maximum depth is 83 feet. The loch became a National Nature Reserve in 1964 so there are no sporting facilities – unless you count fishing as a sport. The loch is the largest freshwater loch in the Lowlands and in the Top Twenty for size in the country.

A road runs from Ballingry to Scotlandwell, crossing the cut at the New Gullet Bridge, then the Old Gullet Bridge over the original outflow. Beyond is Lochend, which now lies well away from the end of the loch. Scotlandwell sits on the higher ground on the far side of this expanded valley. All the towns down the River Leven perch high on the banks as the river was prone to flooding in the days before the controls. With all that went into the river from the mills (there were over thirty) the Leven was known in those days as the filthiest river in Scotland.

The day was summer hot, having furled earlier cloud sails, and with a fiery sun I set off with poor expectations but managed, almost completely, to cover the distance walking field edges rather than road. This is not an easier, softer, quicker option but guarantees survival, which I'm quite keen on. Roads are fine when minutes pass traffic free, but here it was cars per minute, rather than minutes per car. I made a clockwise road circuit to cut the anti-clockwise border line and then followed the road up and over and along down to Auchmuir Bridge. In every other field in the valley bottom tractors were busy bringing in the harvest. The fields beside the road had all been harvested so were stubble (in one field newly limed) and gave the alternative walking. There is a gamble in doing this: one may reach the end of a big field and find no gate or way back onto the road or into the next field. I was only caught out once and using an old trick, climbed over by a well-positioned sycamore! On one occasion I noticed a huddle of eight pheasants in their untidy reconditioning state. Overhead, like a silent raptor, was the last glider I'd see. The Scottish Gliding Centre, Portmoak, lies beside this end of Loch Leven. Braehead School where I taught in the sixties 'did' gliding, so I was able to go up, a wonderful experience over my home landscape, but taking in more and more of the world, as we soared into silence and wheeled the world on a wingtip. The gliders looked so frail and gangly on the ground but once aloft they became as beautiful as birds.

For some decades I'd a brother living beside the River Leven down from Auchmuir Bridge so I'd walked the river often, a pleasing river, whispering along and occasionally clearing its throat at a weir. The path was very overgrown, perhaps fewer fishermen these days from the River Leven Fishing Club. What surprised me at Auchmuir Bridge was encountering three varicoloured alpacas who stood with that strange, concentrated, stare, following my every move. Their names were Boris, Bongo and Alphonso.

Nearing Leslie, a new footpath directed the way up to town from *behind* the first houses. A Scotways sign indicated routes: back the way to Auchmuir Bridge and, by crossing the river, to Bloody Foots and Flowers of May. The road curving down from the centre of Leslie crosses the Leven by Cabbagehall Bridge to the Sparrow Braes (the name appears in Blaeu, one of the earliest maps showing Scotland) to the contiguous Glenrothes suburbs of Newcastle and Macedonia, the former below the Goatmilk Hills.

(How's that for an assemblage of names?) Riverside Park runs right through the sprawl of Glenrothes.

The new, rising path took me up to the Prinlaws end of Leslie where Devine's Café, new to me, was a godsend. Drinks and a chocolate brownie. I'd become quite dehydrated. As a bonus a bus then turned up and I started the two hours of buses required to reach home, *Magudi* keeping me happy. I found it weird to be so immersed in Indian life, while the Fife landscape slipped by. Early morning dew had given me wet feet again, so off came the trainers in the bus for appreciated toe-wiggling. My socks did not smell all that bad.

The Bishop

I want air, and sunshine and blue sky,
The feeling of breezes upon my face,
The feeling of turf beneath my feet.
And no walls but the far mountain tops.
Then I am free, and strong.

Longfellow

Or, as Robert Louis Stevenson sang, 'All I seek, the heaven above/And the road below me'. I was back on the trail early as the forecast was for a hot afternoon once mist had dispersed. There was much uphill to cover at the start, too much on tarmac or hard farm tracks. I reminded myself, 'Slow and easy goes far in a day'. The clouds were down, but clouds with promise in them, so the coolness was welcomed. Loch Leven fills a sort of natural basin, rimmed with hills and, curiously, so does the interior of the Lomonds. The county's Border roughly divides the Lomonds into two parts with the Fife, east, lower part filled with reservoirs

(Holl, Ballo, Harperleas), the west Kinross ground sloping up gently, to reach a dramatic scarp, and plunge down to the Loch Leven world. Just after the mist finally lifted a girl of about ten, standing on the rim, turned from her father to spread her arms like wings and shout, "I'm on top of the world". (Maybe she'd seen the film *Titanic*.) Local poet Michael Bruce called what she saw, 'the goodly scene'. One of the key reasons we summit hills, is to be exalted by the view. I often played the game of keeping eyes on the ground while ascending and only looking up at the summit for the sudden frizz of wonder. Arriving in mist and rain can never reward so well, though when the weather is really bad, there are the rewards of accomplishment. At heart, we want the kind old sun, we want the warm feeling of being on top of the world, of sharing the magic when laughing is heard on the hill.

I'm rather getting ahead of myself. I was back in Leslie (once Fettykil) early and rarin' to go. The Border goes up directly from Auchmuir Bridge but was not practical, so I took the parallel Strathenry Avenue by The Hazels for the Holl Reservoir. Drives to the Strathenry demesne head off to the west. The house is old, the tower older, and there would have been residences before that. Mary Queen of Scots dined at the house on the way to Falkland in April 1563 and one wonders if she went over or round the Lomonds to do so. In the early C18 a three year old was snatched from outside the door of the house and carried off by gypsies. They were soon hunted down and the child recovered. He had been on a visit from home in Kirkcaldy, his name Adam Smith his fame, later, as the author of *The Wealth of Nations*. At one time, long ago, nearby Strathenry paid the monastery on Inchcolm 1000 eels, 2 pigs and 1 cow annually.

At the end of the two mile rise signposts pointed in several directions (the Lomonds offer endless interesting walks), my route westwards, was on tracks at a kindly angle. I still took to field edges. A prim farm was passed, then I picked up the Holl Burn, a cheery companion beside the road. On reaching a wood I had a pause and sat back against a tree, the burn bubbling beside me, right on the Fife–Kinross Border. The wood was signed Lapin Loup Wood – why this combination of French, Scots and English in the name? There were some unusual toadstools but I'm like most walkers, always intending to learn about them, and never doing so. Appreciation will have to suffice. I did look at lichens on my beech tree, whose names too are eminently forgettable Latin tags. Mature beech trees marked the burnside. Walking on, I was puzzled at there seemingly being two Tongue Burns on the map, but I noted there was a one-time cut feeding one round to the other; Kinross stealing water from reaching Fife's Holl Reservoir to take it to their Arnot Reservoir. The stream starts just 200 feet below the summit of the Bishop.

West Feal (pro. Fail) has to be one of the highest farms in Fife: must make for a challenging life sometimes in winter. There was a disembodied calling of geese flying south, presumably above the moving mists, voices I was hearing every day. Forest lay ahead, the large spread of Munduff Hill. The track edged the forest, with a row of statuesque mature beeches, then a planting of youthful oak, before going up a green (dewy-wet) corridor between

Japanese larch, which were taking on their golden autumn tints. While peching up the forest the cloud had rolled away briefly and, on popping out, West Lomond stood boldly to the north; in Fife. There was an area where the ground was all humps and bumps from old limestone quarries, what, in Somerset, they call 'gruffy ground'. A large herd of brown cows and calves had gathered near a feeder and their scent wafted with me all the way to the rim. This landscape is a world of its own, seeming endless miles of green plateau. Without the clear tracks, navigation would have been a challenge. A signpost pointed back the way to Holl, ahead to Glen Vale and, left for Kinnesswood. A geodesic 'golf ball' looked as if sitting *on* the trees, the supporting structure hidden. In the mist it looked surreal, as if a door would open and men from Mars step out.

Then, suddenly there was a glider-high view, gained through hard sweat on my part rather than convenient thermals. Loch Leven filled the basement view. The track doubles back over the rim to descend to Easter Balgedie in a series of zig zags, the maximum surely for any tracked vehicle. This must be a very old right-of-way from Leslie to the plateau workings and down to the loch. From the top of the track looking north I spotted Carlin Maggie, a pinnacle under a band of crags. The crags were also once quarried. On my earliest visit to the Lomonds as a boy, Carlin Maggie was taller with a wee stone 'toorie' on top which later fell off.

The OS map shows a unique symbol running down the slope, looking like a hairy caterpillar, which was named as the Scothart

Row, while along a bit, south, was Kinnesswood Row. All my life I'd been puzzled by the 'row' feature and now really set about trying to find out what they were. Book after book failed to even mention the quarrying which was once such a large activity, and the remains of which are still seen. At last I came on one brief mention. Apparently seams of limestone, eight to twenty feet deep, were found on the Bishop and quarried, the stone carted to the west face and thrown down the 'rows', then, by 'slipes' (sledges), drawn to the kilns. Snoddy's *Afoot in Fife* is a bit more detailed. The word rhymes with 'how' and, in local parlance, the stones were 'rowed' down the slope. In one instance the board to hold a cart in place on the cliff edge broke and cart and horse, 'were rowed doon the brae'. One of Michael Bruce's poems mentions the activities, so it was certainly happening in the mid C18.

In 1852 a report of gold being found on the Bishop led to a gold rush, with thousands swarming over the slopes, but the result was more Charlie Chaplin than reality, for the excitement had been started by someone discovering *pyrites* – fool's gold. When I found my first as a boy, I too had thought I'd struck it rich, only to be quickly disillusioned.

I'd left Fife's Border down below West Feal and would only meet it again when crossing Glen Vale. Kinross, on the far shore of Loch Leven, is that county's only town, so squeezed in between the snaring M90 and the Kinross House lands, that Kinross now almost encaptures Milnathort. Castle Island is obvious and a few other markers are worth picking out.

Kinross House, with impressive gardens, was built to look out to Castle Island; the house, gardens, loch, old castle, hills beyond, all making an inspired whole, thanks to Sir William Bruce, who designed the site in the late C17. Kinross was Scotland's first great classical country mansion. Defoe recorded it as 'the most beautiful and regular piece of architecture in all Scotland'. Bruce had been involved in the negotiations with Charles II leading to the Restoration in 1660 and became the royal architect. He worked on Holyrood Palace in Edinburgh, though the King never visited.

In 1742 a new church was planned in Kinross, but there was no steeple proposed. Many people were so offended at this seeming slight they set about funding a steeple. And there sits their steeple but no church, a change of plan having that built elsewhere. Churches without steeples are common, a steeple without a church is rare.

Traffic on the M90 was catching the sun and twinkling like a drape of fairy lights. There was only the faintest buzz from the traffic. A breeze acted as silencer and chilled me. Autumn was marching on. A wave to Kinross and the Ochils and I moved on.

The path along the rim was edged by a newish fence, a decayed fence and a half-sunken wall. (How many centuries does that triple constructing record?) I left it to go up the bump with a cairn on top that is the highest point of the Bishop (461m, 1512ft). The name covers the area rather than just the pimply summit. This was Bishopshire (just as Benarty was in Lochoreshire), once the barony of the Archbishop of St Andrews. Play golf at Kinnesswood? Head to the Bishopshire Golf Club.

Kinnesswood, Scotlandwell, East and West Balgedie; the villages lying at the foot of this western Lomond's scarp and above the land reclaimed by the lowering of Loch Leven, are particularly attractive, with deep, narrow lanes, some cobbled, cottages with pantiles, and old and new dwellings, quite randomly mixed without destroying the singular charm. Old tracks climb up onto the Bishop from the hamlets. The villages come under Portmoak parish and the parish church sits by the road just along from Scotlandwell. The minister in the early C18 was Ebeneezer Erskine, a notable preacher, who might preach in the open air to gatherings of 2,000 people. He was one of many ministers who resented patronage and thought congregations should be the ones to choose their shepherd. Erskine was 'called' by the Kinross church but they had another man thrust upon them. The congregation barred the unwanted man's entry and in the end the Black Watch from Perth were called in. Eventually a group from the area met at the Gairney Bridge (SW corner of Loch Leven) in 1712 and formed the breakaway, Secession Church. An obelisk (1733) marks the spot today. Scotland aye took matters of faith maist seriously.

Michael Bruce, a weaver's son, was born in Kinnesswood in 1746 and enjoyed some repute as a poet, but died of TB at the age of twenty one. His birthplace is a small museum. The meteorologist Dr Buchan was also from here and was the detector of the 'Buchan Cold Spells' in our weather (They occur on each 7-10 Feb, 11-14 Apr, 29 Jun – 4 July, 6-11 Aug, 6-12 Nov ,if you want to check them out).

Andrew Wynton, Prior of St Serf's, is recalled as an early historian, *The Oryginale Cronykill* telling our story from the creation of the world almost up to his own death in the reign of James I (of Scotland). St Serf's Island, the largest in Loch Leven, sits in its SE corner, completely flat and with almost nothing to show of past history. A Pictish king granted the island to the Culdees in C8 and they were there for 400 years before being supplanted by Augustinian monks. Scotlandwell is the site of a rather special well. The large canopied basin has a sandy bottom from which the cool water bubbles up. Kids find this fascinating. There's a cup on a chain so one can drink from a spout. Robert the Bruce was supposedly a visitor in his later years when he was suffering from some skin disease. The Romans must have marched this way for this is their 'Fons Scotiae' of Tacitus.

Loch Leven was once famed for curling, a game played by the monks of St Serf's Island, and an association (club) was active by 1651. Today, curling is pursued almost entirely indoors. I wonder when Loch Leven was last used for curling, the gatherings for which had the resonant title, Bonspiel. Global warming again? Winters certainly are not what they were. In the seventies I tried to garner as many winter Munros as possible on ski and had a good decade doing so but, almost imperceptibly, the rate began to drop because the snow conditions were failing to make ascents worthwhile. Another pointer. When I was a boy, a farmer would flood a field or two by the River Devon, to make an open air skating venue. The school had two statutory 'skating halves' when classes were suspended and town and gown headed for an afternoon on the ice. When visiting the Dollar Museum recently I asked a senior pupil there about this tradition. He knew nothing of it; the tradition, the half days off classes, had gone before his time.

At school I'd come on a song with the words, 'Up in the Lomonds I lay, I lay/ And watched the castles a-burning all day, all day' which tickled my fancy, for Castle Campbell above Dollar was one of those suffering the ravaging by Montrose as he marched along the Hillfoots in 1645. From up there I could see the Lomonds and imagined the smokes going up along the Ochils. So I cycled along and went up Glen Vale onto West Lomond to put the song into right ordering. Castle Campbell was the Edinburgh town house for the Campbells. One historian suggested that this was as near Edinburgh as they'd risk sleeping overnight.

Castle Campbell came to the first Earl of Argyll by marriage and he had the name changed from the Gloum by Act of Parliament. The castle still perches above the meeting of the Burn of Care and the Burn of Sorrow, facing Gloum Hill. The second earl was killed at Flodden (who wasn't?) and two later earls were executed, the eighth earl in 1661 after the Restoration. He had been responsible for the execution of the Marquis of Montrose who had defeated him in the Battles of Inverkeithing and Kilsyth (1645). Montrose and his Highlanders ravaged the Hillfoots but were in too much of a hurry to take the castle. The castle came to the National Trust for Scotland in 1948 but is administrated by Historic Scotland. As a boy I came to know the solitary mason who both lived and worked on site. Somewhere in the structure is a stone I was allowed to finish off with a chisel and mallet.

The miles on to Glen Vale always seem longer, heading over "plenty of nothing" in the words of one of the cyclists I met. I must have encountered a score of groups or individuals in the day and half of them were with, sometimes even on, mountain bikes, all were chatty and friendly, all just too pleased to escape awhile from the stifling restrictions of urban life. This was where renewal lay.

I both enjoyed and disliked my lengthy, complex commuting journeys to and from the Border line each day. Boredom only came with the repetitive sections and then I escaped to other worlds, in books. This day ended with three different bus routes and no quick connections between them, repeated the next day with the demanding slog up from Easter Balgedie to continue the sprawl of the Bishop.

West Lomond

Life is short, the mountain infinitely high,
but the route goes on.
W. H. Murray.

If ever a day had ups and downs, this was classic. The Bishop was blowy. On a glider flight from Portmoak years ago I had had 'lift' explained to me, and the great benefit from that steep, very steep western face of the Lomonds I'd just toiled up. Basically, warm air was sent upwards to create high-rise thermals. Today, the wind rushing up over the edge had a surf-like roar and any glider would have gone tumbling up skyward and back to earth, miles away in many pieces. The wind was strong enough that I was constantly almost tripping myself up, with one leg being flung in front of the other by the gusts. I would have enjoyed the tussle normally, but was woefully clad for such wind and the resulting windchill. The forecast had been for the cloud to lift for another sunny afternoon so I saved weight and left out a windcheater. Heat generated by moving only just sufficed to continue. Not a time to break a leg. Thank goodness the Lomond paths and tracks are so prominent. I scurried along in the gloom of the curdled clouds. Rain would have killed me but I lived to write another day.

The route soon turned down 'inland' and fences and gates and features came as expected. There was one brief clearance, with East Lomond bold and with colourful dots of walkers down on the Harperleas track. East and West Lomond, in folklore, became 'Wallace's Goals' as it was deemed the hero was capable of jumping from one to the other.

This is a strange area of the Lomonds with the slope all complex ridges and hollows and, surprisingly, some trees, too varied (some deciduous) to have been a failed plantation. I was granted another cloud break on the final steep track down, but had already decided Glen Vale, Fife boundary as it was, could wait for another day. I feel its features are rather over-rated anyway, with a scruffy cave, a wee waterfall, and John Knox's Pulpit, not a patch on the Bunnet Stane, and that to be reached over the highest spot in Fife, West Lomond (522m, 1713ft).

Studying the map and considering transport logistics the decision had really been made the night before. The Fife boundary makes two illogical jags into Kinross's farming landscape which would have been tricky for pedestrian progress, so cutting across the base of these, south-north would be an easier option and take in West Lomond on a traverse rather than an up-down if continuing down Glen Vale. I was also curious as to where Kinross-shire became Perthshire and was initially non-plussed that all the maps I looked at did not show a boundary; of course, now it is just part of the 'unitary authority' of Perth and Kinross. (Now that is rather curious: Kinnesswood and Rannoch Station connected!) The apex of the more northerly Fife jag would hardly have been walkable, being on the M90 in the motorway cutting through to Glenfarg. But that is where Kinross's county boundary once headed west, along the Ochils to the Dunning road. After today my Fife Boundary wiggles uncomplainingly north east and, throughout, is the march with Perthshire.

Neither of my Victorian gazetteers of 1832 and 1882 mentions the name Glen Vale, which is a sort of tautology, but the anglicized Vale is probably just a corruption of some earlier word.

As a teenager I was rather put out at the name John Knox's Pulpit for I doubted the reformer would ever have been there. He doesn't mention the site in his autobiography. The hunted Covenanters were certainly there, holding illegal conventicles and listening to impassioned preachers. The pockmarked rock face holding the 'pulpit' helps with the acoustics. I recall on one occasion giving my own teenage presentation of Psalm 23 from the spot, fortunately just to an assemblage of sheep. One old diary tells of a 1678 preaching in the glen with a large crowd gathered to hear the Rev. John Dickson preach, but the meeting broke up and people fled when a watchman had blown his horn to warn of approaching dragoons.

That is straightforward enough but some facts can become marvellously entwined with legend. At a conventicle on the Lomonds in 1674, with one John Wellwood the preacher, 'there came a party of lifeguards under Masterton of Grange Younger, who fired upon the gathering several times but caused no injury among the gathered men, women and children.' That sounds remarkable but at the same time several women who had remained at home claimed that they had seen a vision of a majestic figure poised in the air over the gathering at the time of the attack.

In the valley, quite a distinct east-west pass, I received a distinct whiff of cigarette smoke yet there was no one in sight for at least 400 yards upwind. From the track through the valley bottom I knew a clear path headed up into the murk directly to West Lomond. (The scar can be seen from the Bishop.) Why walkers tackle a steep slope directly like that is a mystery and, doing so, inevitably leads to a hideously eroded line. The popular approach track to West Lomond from the east, curls round the cone of hill to gain the summit from the west, a track created in an effort to heal the scar on the east face. But many ignore it, and that eastern scar is as ugly as ever I'm told.

I worked up through heather, for much of the northern plateau, Fife's part of the Lomonds is as much heather as poor grass, contrasting with the green grass of Kinross's Bishop. Often green points to underlying limestone. There is odd terracing and my path took me up to a bank where this flank was bare and gritty along some length. Being so dry the slope was dotted with clumps of bell heather which were still in bold flower, while the ling only showed pale remnants in what was a sea of past-flowering grey. Along lay the Devil's Burdens, a small outcrop of weathered rock. The story goes that the Devil was having a confrontation with one Maggie (a witch?) and he dropped the burden of stones he was carrying to chase her and turn her into stone: the Carlin Maggie noted earlier. On the plateau edge north of the Devil's Burden I noticed the name Wind and Weather which I thought highly appropriate.

The slightly horizontal ridge I was on allowed me to lie prone below the wind level and I enjoyed watching, through my binoculars, a party heading up for the Bishop on the track I'd come down. They appeared and disappeared as the clouds blew past and finally vanished. I heard a noise behind me and turned, expecting to see a sheep perhaps, only to have a biker loom over me and shoot off along the bare crest. I don't know who had the bigger surprise. Descending that flank of the hill must be about the ultimate steepness for a bike. I almost envied him. In my teens and later I cycled everywhere, every holiday, on a sturdy old bike with the luxury of a Sturmy Archer three-speed gear. I took 'Umslopogaas' (named after a Rider Haggard hero) places cycles were never meant to go. We knew our exploring as rough stuff cycling. What changes technology has brought to every sport and pastime – and what harder challenges have resulted.

The grassy slope was not a friendly texture to wander on, so I just went up the scar, slowly, keeping a steady pace and steady breathing; what I was taught as 'floating up'. Bullied up this day, I needed the physical demand to counter the piercing wind, which felt as if cutting through clothing to chill bones and marrow. A stile crossed a fence running across the slope, but had been built right below a small spring so the upper access was black, liquid bog. I crossed the fence instead, as everyone was doing judging by the state of the strands, and muttered something about someone's lack of 'gumption'. There was one brief easing of the angle and then another which, surprisingly, was onto the summit flat with trig and cairn not far ahead.

The trig was set in a concrete base and this whole structure was undercut, presumably eroded in what was, in geological time, but recently. The cairn was once a large burial cairn, probably Neolithic (4000 – 700BC), and digs found bones and an urn. I reached the trig over several hollow circles in the hummock of stones which are a puzzle as to origin or purpose. Oddly, East Lomond (434m, 1471ft) was chosen for the Great Ordnance Survey. Thomas Carlyle and Edward Irving visited the camp, where they found half a dozen hefty tents, a 'black-stained' cook tent, and a pile of coal. Too bright a day for work, they were shown the theodolite and looked at the shimmering marker on Ben Lomond, 60 miles west.

I dropped down the lee side just far enough to gain some shelter from the boisterous wind and relished much-needed food and drink. No trying to pinpoint faraway Lochnagar today. A female runner loomed up from the east's steep slope, gave me a wave and headed down again over to my left on what I took to be the western path, which I was soon happy to follow. I was surprised how steep it was. Suddenly there was a complete break in the clouds below my level and for a while the landscape looked startingly unfamiliar. I sat to pore over the maps (I carried both OS 25 and 50 thousand) and to pinpoint both Gateside, my destination on the A91, and how and where to descend to the rock curiosity of the Bunnet Stane. The lass, and now I, were not on the circuit path, but on a path straight down the north side of the mountain cone, one not shown on a map. (These maps' path delineation was hardly of the best.) Beyond Gateside lay the sprawl of the lowering end of the Ochils through which the Border ran and I spent a long time studying possible ways through the more agricultural lower slopes. I ended annotating fields on my map as an aid: gr. (green; grass), br (brown: ploughed or bare), and yel. (yellow: where grain had been harvested). Gates would determine choices ultimately but at least the fields were not edged with ditches as on the River Leven side of the Lomonds (they often were, I'd find). I rather like the way Fife's two main rivers top and tail the Lomonds.

The busy A91 east-west through the Howe is paralleled by an older Dryside road that runs from Strathmiglo round to Loch Leven and no doubt had earned the name at one time. Strathmiglo, Gateside and Burnside milestoned the A91, the burn of the last being some of the founding waters of the River Eden. The intensity of farming has effaced many prehistoric sites once in the Howe, but in the early C19 a Rev. Andrew Small, who'd retired to Edenshead, (Gateside's big house), combed the area and became convinced of many Roman forts and camps and older burials. Above all, this was the site, down by the Urquhart farms, where Calgacus faced them in the battle of Mons Graupius! All my life I have lived in hope that some archaeological miracle will find just where that battle was fought. The reverend alone suggests this area.

I took easy angles down. As the direct path was lethally slippery, I used trods to reach the path that went over the rim and steeply down to the Bunnet Stane. This used the complexities of the slope admirably and I'm sure must have been a route going back millennia. Prehistoric people lived on the Lomonds after all and must have travelled. A pathside boulder was polished, presumably by patting hands or 'skarting' sheep and that didn't happen in a day. I relished the descent, but greeted a couple ascending with, "Aye, a sair pech". Ah, the vagaries of maps; the 1:25,000 splattered names on the site (Dow Craig, Maiden Bore, Cave, Bunnet Stane) but did not show the path down, the 1:50,000 showed the path but gave no mention of the site.

The rocks of the Bunnet Stane site are one of several similar chunks along the foot of the hill and have survived to the present by being a harder sandstone than layers above them. I first came on the fenced, but gated entrance of the cave which is, more correctly, a rectangular chamber, the Maiden's Bower, carved out by man, when and why open to speculation. Above lies the Maiden Bore and then, round and up, the extraordinary Bunnet Stane. The

Bore is a hole through the rock and thought, anciently, only to be passable by 'maidens' (virgins) though the girth of maidens generally seems to make the passage impossible now. The Bunnet Stane is a 'dining table for eight'-sized slab of rock perched on a pedestal. 'Like a huge mushroom.' Legend says that anyone who leaps onto it from the nearby rock is going to be a hero (or dead). The Maiden's Bower has a traditional story which I thought fell short on invention. The bower was the meeting place for two young lovers, a state of affairs not approved of by her father who had his men lie in wait and murder the young man as he made for the rendezvous. The maiden then vowed never to return home and lived out her life here, doing good, and finally recognised as a saint. Snoddy had another version, from a local shepherd, where the girl fled to the site to escape the plague. Alas, the lover lad couldn't resist visiting and brought the fatal infection with him.

The clouds obeyed the forecast and, at three o'clock grey skies turned to blue with dashes of white. Pleasant paths led northwards between fields to meet the minor Dryside road, from which a tarmac Station Road broke off to lead to Gateside. A small bridge crosses the young River Eden which rises a few miles west, on the watershed with the Loch Leven basin. In times past this was the River Miglo, only becoming the Eden at Strathmiglo. The haws in the hedgerow were bright scarlet and patches of white dead nettle were still in flower.

Gateside is a hamlet in a twist of A91 where the A912 breaks off for Glenfarg and Perth. A hoped for pub had gone. Buses came every two hours and I was there with a 45 minute wait before my final run home. The sun came out but when it went behind a cloud the tiptoeing breeze still felt cool. I sat on a wall, then walked along the row of cottages to the village hall and back. The tiny gardens had been left to themselves and there were amazing shows of pink nerines and scarlet or white *Schizostylis* (Kaffir Lily). The latter, the books noted were from South Africa, and not too hardy yet my first view of them – in cheery flower – had been in Lerwick, under winter snow. They are one of my favourite flowers, brightening up the gloom of the year's end.

I said hello to some shaggy ponies at the entrance to Edenshead House. One of the previous owners had been Robert Philp, founder of schools and a Kirkcaldy philanthropist. My last bus home would pass the Philp Hall.

Gateside has a story of Covenanting times. Following a West Lomond raid a trooper banged on one door in order to search for fugitives. (A covenanter was hidden 'ben the hoose'.) The knock was answered by a weird woman with tangled hair and ragged garb, who shouted curses at the soldier and made as if to attack him. The trooper had expected to see some old, frightened creature, not this apparition. When the woman screamed, "Do you expect to find someone in Hell?" the terrified trooper fled thinking he'd encountered a witch.

I finished off all the nibbles and juice I had, scattering some crumbs for the birds, a picnic habit I had started a lifetime ago after reading Robert Louis Stevenson so doing in his wanderings through the Cevennes. A black-headed gull (black head a grey smudge) tentatively approached then gave me a polite bow.[6] I could hardly refuse, could I? Two jackdaws had been watching and flew down hoping for some crumbs but they would not come really close while the gull held the field.

Time for the bus. Walking along, I discovered my bus pass had gone. A frantic search. Rucksack rummaged. A race to where I'd sat at the corner, over to the ponies, along the street to the last town stop. My card was definitely lost. There was nothing like the losing of my pass to make me realise its value. I made Kirkcaldy just in time to go into the Town House and set procedures going to receive a new one. That business is farmed out to somewhere in England and I was told a new card could take up to a week to reach me. The week proved nineteen days. Fortunately, the following morning a lady in Gateside rang me to say she had found my card and would post it to me. (I had a small sticker on the card giving my name and telephone number, for just this contingency. I recommend the practice!)

Jenny Nettles, some sources say, was a Strathmiglo lass who was wooed by one of Rob Roy's men who were based in Falkland during the Fifteen Rising. She was 'got with child' but was abandoned when the Macgregors departed. She fled up into the Lomonds with her bairn and 'was never seen no more'. Some sources say she hanged herself. I wonder what sad reality lies behind this sad, angry, anonymous song? (Oxter is *armpit*.)

---

6 Immature gulls make a hunched sort of bow to a parent bird when begging for food.

JENNY NETTLES

Saw ye Jenny Nettles,
Jenny Nettles, Jenny Nettles,
Saw ye Jenny Nettles
Coming frae the Market;
Bag and Baggage on her Back,
Her Fee and Bountith in her Lap;
Bag and Baggage on her Back,
And a Babie in her Oxter.

I met ayont the Kairny,
Jenny Nettles, Jenny Nettles,
Singing till her Bairny,
Robin Rattles' Bastard;
To feel the Dool upo' the Stool,
And ilka ane that mocks her,
She round about seeks Robin out,
To stap it in his Oxter.

Fy, fy! Robin Rattle,
Robin Rattle, Robin Rattle;
Fy, Fy! Robin Rattle,
Use Jenny Nettles kindly:
Score out the Blame, and shun the Shame,
And without mair Debate o't,
Take hame your Wain, make Jenny fain,
The leal and leesome Gate o't.

Chapter Five

HOWE TO TAY

The stars I look at
Died millions of years ago.
So thanks for coming.

Above the Howe of Fife

THE HOURS SPENT in buses were beginning to pall (today's tally was nearly five hours) but the sun shone so benignly that I largely just sat looking at the good landscape, *Malgudi* forgotten. My first bus, as night drained away, had been 0731 to Kirkcaldy, from whence an 0800 to Glenrothes, arriving 0851. My third bus was not till 0935 so, with Gregg's offering a roll and drink for £2.65 I sat in the sun making the most of the deal: coffee and a crispy bacon roll. And some more pages read of skulduggery in *Malgudi*. My final bus, destination Kinross by Loch Leven, a route normally served by a small vehicle had a double decker provided. I had the bus to myself and sat upstairs to watch Fife slip by. Quite a tour.

We just touched the hem of Falkland, snuggling in below East Lomond (Falkland Hill), famed for a royal palace and town of antique character. Freuchie was the first straggling village. Nobody climbed on board. Freuchie still lives on the fame of 1985 when their cricket team beat Rowledge at Lords to win the British Village Cricket Trophy. (Imagine an away game in Somerset.) Cricket does have an enthusiastic following in Scotland. I'd uncles and cousins who played for Fife County when I was a boy. I enjoyed playing at school in a gung-ho fashion and found cricket boots with their studs were perfect for gripping the steep, grassy flanks of the Ochils. If Freuchie's achievement is surprising, let's not forget Scotland beat England in 2018 in a 50-overs match: England 365 all out (Bairstow 105), Scotland 371 for 5 (MacLeod 140 not out, with just seven balls remaining). That was exciting. Need I add that neither feat has been repeated?

The bus then sped on to Dunshalt, a one-street village rooted in the Howe of Fife, and so to Auchtermuchty which could be designated as a small town. The Muchty's most famous resident was the magical musician Jimmy Shand. There's a fine statue of Sir Jimmy standing, life size, playing his accordion. Some claim they have seen his foot tapping to a faint whispering of music.

Fife enjoys a good share of couthy names like Auchtermuchty. There's an old rhyme saying 'Largo, Blebo, Dunino/ Into Europe seems to go,/ But plainly Scottish we may deem/ Auchtermuchty, Pittenweem'.

Besides Auchtermuchty and Auchmuir Bridge, Fife also has Auchtertool and Auchterderran (and Auchtermairnie Farm). *Auch* is one of the Gaelic elements in place names meaning piece of land, a landholding perhaps. *Muc* is pig. Approaching Auchtermuchty from Dunshalt, no contour line would be crossed in an hour if walking east. Until drained in mid-C18 this flat was Loch Rossie.

The bus does a circular through Strathmiglo which can, briefly, un-nerve new passengers thinking they are heading in the wrong direction. Along the Eden's wide upper valley, the road is dominated to the south by the shapely twin peaks and wide body of the Lomonds. To the north, the harlequin clothing of intense farming leads up the braes of what are still the Ochils, though few think about them as such. They are often written as North Fife Hills. But Ochils is true: the OS says so!

There's an old weather rhyme about the Howe that assured me today's weather would be alright: 'When Falkland Hill puts on her cap,/ The Howe of Fife will get a drap;/ And when the Bishop draws his coul,/ Look out for wind and weather foul'. Another notes, 'Mist on the hills weather spills;/ Mist in the howes weather grows', and one I'm more aware of, living on the Fife coast: 'When the mist comes to the hills,/ Ye'll get water for your mills;/ When the mist comes from the sea,/ Fair weather it will be'. I liked the stolid certainty of today's weather described as 'stationery'. Reassuring, unlike a forecast from Chuck Palaniuk (USA): 'Just for the record, the weather today is pretty suspicious with chances of betrayal.'

When descending from West Lomond to Gateside I had studied options for following the erratic Border onwards and upwards but, studying the maps at home, I realised I could take the bus two miles further to Burnside for a less problematic route, which was also the exact line of the Border. Maybe I should have had suspicions. I was to be betrayed.

One small statistic however; I crossed the Perthshire Border six times today. A single mile of this Border (down to Pittuncarty) lies in Perthshire as the Border does a loop. I wondered about road maintenance for quirks like that. Does Fife stop surfacing, for instance, for that section? Do Perthshire lorries trundle through

Fife to reach their wee bit? I'm sure this thinking went back to the Sixties when I often skied at the Cairnwell and the road condition over the great pass was something of a joke, one side so much better than the other: we drove to the pass from Perthshire (the Devil's Elbow in those years) but used Braemar/Aberdeenshire accommodation, thus observing both council's efforts. On the pass the demarcation was unmistakable, a wee bump and a quite different surface. And snowploughs of course only went up *their* side of the pass, so you could have folk from the south ski-ing while those from Deeside were unable to reach the Cairnwell – or vice versa.

The one-man bus tour duly terminated at Burnside on the Fife Border. From there a track headed up onto the heights in a remarkably straight line. The track had a name, Yellowhill Road, and Yellow Hill, 197m lay just off the road's high point. The start appeared to be a track from the west end of Burnside up a tiny stream (off the main stream) lined with odd trees, many dead. I found a footpath, not a track, and headed off happily enough until I realised there was something wrong. I was stuck on the main stream. (The map is inadequate I may say in defence.) The path entered a wood and began to lead upwards, towards what the map called Cuthill Towers. Definitely no help for me. A smaller path did drop down to the burn (Border!) so I hoped would lead up to a farm, Bannaty, which lay on the Yellowhill Road. The next hour I'd rather forget.

The burn itself was just the distance that would tempt young adults to leap. There was a barbed wire fence and decayed wall.

To reach it there was what proved a cow pock-marked marsh. Once across I worked upstream a bit, hoping for a field edge to let me gain the Yellowhill Road. Hot, weakening, I stopped to look at the map. My spectacles had gone. I left my rucksack and retraced my course to where I'd crossed the burn (where I'd wet one foot, and then wet the other in the ambushing marsh). No sign of them. That was that then. I carefully searched back to my rucksack and had a third search returning to the burn. "Home James!" Replacing my reading specs was the new priority.

By throwing a couple of rocks in the burn I kept my wet feet dry (in a manner of speaking). And there, where I'd crossed the original fence out of the wood lay my spectacles. So what now? I would suggest that Granny's aphorism that 'no hour is ever wasted' had an exception. I still had to reach the Yellowhill Road.

The simplest option was to retreat to Burnside and use the Bannaty farm road, for there was obviously no track up this way but, 'gey forfochan', I took a quicker option of crossing two or three fields to gain the farm. My feet were already soaked. The first field was well pock-marked with water-filled cattleprints and I half-paddled over to link with the next, which held a herd of beasts. Most of the beasts were lying down, a saner option than mine on such a hot day, and I just skirted them to a gate, and a ploughed field edge up to a final gate onto the Yellowhill Road; at last. A few of the young heifers showed interest as I passed, probably speculating whether I was providing food, but cud-chewing continued peacefully with the rest.

A tractor had stopped and the driver stood ready to take issue with me for 'illegally' going into a field with cows. (Not the law.) I rather think he was slightly nonplussed to face an old gangrel and not some young tearaway. Let him enjoy playing policeman. Too weary to argue, I explained what I was up to (he knew the burn was the Border) but he cut any further conversation, pointed, "Well, that's Yellowhill Road there!" and climbed up onto his colossal machine and went off up ahead of me to then turn off into a field to start spraying silage. Through much of today I was aware of that smell; it seemed to permeate the breeze. I rather like it.

My, the pleasure of putting one foot in front of the other in rhythmic tread again. Obviously I was going to be kept to wee roads and tracks thereafter. Fields were surrounded by impassable fences, sometimes with ditches, sometimes with electrics added, the brown fields were already sown, the green pastures were all being grazed, the yellow were having the last rolls or bales collected. (I'd see huge stores of them at the farms I passed.) Very impressive in a way. But lifeless as far as wildlife went. 'Went' is the word. In my lifetime of country rambling 60% of bird life has gone from our over-laundered fields and woods. (The Swiss chemist who invented DDT was awarded a Nobel Prize.) A racket of rooks far off in one wood, the regular irregular Vs of geese on high, and scrounging crows over the stubbles (I thought of Van Gogh's painting of crows flying over similar fields) were almost all the birdlife seen. The odd clatter of cushies (wood pigeon) too, every day. The swallows had gone and the redwings were yet to come.

There was one special moment when a 'charm' of goldfinches made their companionable way high above the roadside trees. Passing through. They're *gowdpink* in a Burns poem. Apart from the dove, the goldfinch is the most portrayed bird in Renaissance paintings. I recall going to the National Gallery in Edinburgh in December 2016 to queue to see the iconic painting of a goldfinch by Carel Fabritius, regarded as Rembrandt's greatest pupil. *The Goldfinch* (1654) was on tour with just seven weeks in Scotland. The artist was killed at the age of 32 when a massive gunpowder explosion wrecked a part of Delft and destroyed his studio so few works survive. The Victorians almost wiped out the goldfinch as a UK species from keeping them in cages.

All day, nothing four-footed, with fur or prickles, crossed my road or lay pancaked as carkill. But why should they have been on land ruled for yield and profit where man, on his high perch, has lifted himself above the soil? I noticed an interesting comment on this a while back where a farmer was surprised to be told his land had been invaded by the New Zealand flat worm (which eats our beneficial earthworms). The discovery was made by a man walking his dog. The farmer had to admit he had not set foot on that field in years; everything was done by tractor and, up there, one did not notice worms in the soil.

At the crest by Yellow Hill I had a restorative break. A Scotways sign pointed back the way I'd come. What I was discovering was a bit of country with exceptional views. Over the years, motoring from Perth into Fife, I would choose the minor road over the eastern Ochils to descend Glentarkie simply for the sudden revelationary view of the Lomond hills. Now here I was, with a whole day of that bounteousness granted by being on foot. For once I accepted, gracefully, the walking of unavoidable tarmac, even under a sun which was more than just warm.

When the slopes of the huge southern fields rose more steeply, the land became more complex and there were many stands of trees and woods, both conifers and deciduous, making for ever-changing features. The land itself was rolling, warty, till on the furthest slopes the vast Pitmedden Forest took over. Four roads went over the hills: the twisty Glen Farg[7] one now overwhelmed by the M90, the A912 from Gateside to lower Glen Farg and Perth, the Glentarkie – Abernethy minor road north from Strathmiglo and the B936 from Auchtermuchty to Lindores and Newburgh. Between the first three of these, some minor roads run east-west, as convoluted as the land. On or off, these roads were the prosperous farms, often turned into near hamlets in themselves, with huge barns and amazing machinery. Farming appears to be a high-tech branch of engineering and chemistry nowadays, an industry rather than a stewardship of the land.

Not long into my roadwalking I came to Newton of Balconquhal, almost a hamlet, where the farm had added houses. There was the big house and other nicely-named places nearby: Blindwell and Summerfield, the whole epitomising the prosperity of the area and enjoying a gift beyond wealth, the view. The

7 Glen Farg has a hostelry in its depths, the Bein Inn. (Maybe you need to be a Scot for the pun). Fife also has a Chance Inn, Drift Inn, Welcome Inn, Step Inn, the Isle of Lewis has an Inn Between and St Kilda, The Puff Inn.

ground fell away attractively to the wide Eden valley and then soared up into the sculptured Lomond Hills, elegant in themselves, both the cones of East and West Lomond catching the sun, while between was the north facing scarp, in secretive shadow. Alan Paton once described a spot in Natal as 'lovely beyond any singing of it' and I felt that here was 'where essential silence cheers and blesses' (RLS). I almost danced my delight; but we don't, do we, we Scots, for whom 'No bad' is the height of praise?

Looking north the mansion of Balvaird was on a far crest, clean-gleaming white in the sun, the effect spoilt by the slow-turning blades of wind generators behind, also white against a darkening sky. Below, 'cooried doon' in the shadows, was the bulk of Balvaird Castle, louring into Fife. The castle is owned by the Earl of Mansfield (Scone Palace). The family gaining possession by marriage in 1500 when the castle was built. Historic Scotland are guardians.

Sitting to relax by a gate I was forced to move as nosey heifers gathered and I was being given the benefit of their sweet breaths. I'd had my fill of cows already, thank you. In a lifetime of wandering through fields of cows I'd never had any concerns. One is canny of course. I recall a local mountaineering club meet when a couple and I had to go through a field of cattle and I smiled to see one tough climber moving to place his wife between the cows and himself. When I walked the Pennine Way, north to south (which baffled people: 'But it goes south-north') I only met one other person going north-south and he had just had fun with a bull loose in a field crossed by the official Pennine Way (now, *that* is illegal).

The bull came for him and he ran pell-mell to the nearest fence, tumbled over safely, and then lifted his eyes to meet the larger eyes of a docile creature with a big brass ring through his nose. While still a teenager, one summer I was in Oban when the US Navy visited and the Tourist Office was looking for people (kilted if possible) to act as couriers on the bus tours. The pay was negligible but the tips lavish. My route was round Appin, taking in Castle Stalker, Glen Coe, Loch Lomond, Inveraray, Kilchurn Castle and St Conan's Kirk. I was expected to have stories about everything seen and usually did know the facts but, where not, any bloody clan story satisfied. (Or I put Homer in a kilt.) Everything was scribbled down in notebooks and only years later I wondered what a folklorist might make of some of the tales.

That's by the by. In Glen Kinglas there was a herd of Highland cattle on the hillside and there were shouts to stop for photographs. "Say, boy, do all your cows wear winter woollies?" Assured photography was safe, the sailors swarmed up to take their shots. Highlanders are nosey critters and began to wander down. The sailors backed off a bit, the cows came on. In a minute the US Navy was in flight with the meek Highlanders trundling after them. Tips were few that night.

I was tempted to try an Ochil cross-country on a more northerly line, but where it would lead was uncertain and I faced the regular logistical problem of transport home at each days' end so, perforce had to be in striking distance of the A91. My wee road led down to reach the A912, one with all too many cars and lorries per minute, being thwarted twice of hoped-for tracks or a field edge, to cut off what was a down and up section; the first had been built over and the second field was protected by fence and ditch. I must have shared something of the Picts' feelings confronted by Roman defences. The down ended at Upper Pitlochie (why 'upper'; it is pretty well 'doon'?) where I turned uphill on another named road: Leyden Urquhart Road. The names fascinated, hereabouts: Prins Pendicle, Corrinzion, Balcanquhal, Cadgeracre Wood, Pittuncarty.

The road had a ration of potholes with resurfacing, courtesy of cows and sheep, the latter in noisy confrontation, with their handlers at an area of pens and poly-tunnel shelters. This higher level gave a shaggier landscape, fields rolling up to an often wooded skyline. There was a last look at Balvaird Castle, only two fields away, dark and louring as ever. (Defoe reported a rocking stone at the castle in Cromwell's time.) The big house commanded the skyline, the windmills hidden down behind from this angle. I was able to look across the Glentarkie valley to the next day's section, whose route was still speculative but hinted at more fields and dark, impenetrable conifer clumps. A steep short brae from Pittuncarty farm took me down to the Glen Tarkie road. I'd start again from there.

I had a mile and a bit to walk down the road with little traffic passing. Wallander Plantation and Pitlour Park were named, but the glory had departed. I find abandoned walled gardens very sad. On reaching the busy A91, I was pleased to see a pathway led on directly into red stoned Strathmiglo with its beckoning tolbooth steeple.

A few minutes later, by luck rather than planning, I was on a bus (not a double decker) for a rewind tour of Fife, having enjoyed 'one of those rich, ripe days that enlarge one's life' (John Muir). I read *Man Eaters* through to its twist in the tail ending. I'd also brought along another paperback for a re-reading: *The Prisoner of St Kilda*, the strange, true story of the Jacobites' abduction of Lady Grange in 1732. She was subsequently held prisoner in the Western Isles, including St Kilda, from 1734 to 1741. I'm surprised the story hasn't made it as a TV series. At home I had a couple of flowers to look up, one I'd seen several times and thought was a garden escape but was orpine (*Sedum telephium*), called 'midsummer men' in England. The flowers were used on midsummer's eve to test a lover's faithfulness. Two would be stood upright and, in the morning, if leaning towards each other, all was well, if they had fallen apart then so would their hopes.

Today's commonest flowers, usually growing against a wall, had been knapweed, red campion, scabious and dead nettles and, like an indication of past-human presence, nettles or willowherb. As a boy in the 1950s I found one of the last which I thought very pretty and looked up in my flowers book. Willowherb was taking over the bomb sites in London apparently, but was 'a rarity, originating in clearances in Alpine woodlands'. Now the flower is a notorious pandemic spreader. I also had to remove a collection of sticky willie from my pullover sleeves.

Pitmedden Forest

Plant a tree, even though you will never sit under it.

Indian saying.

Glentarkie may come from *torc* which would make this the Wild Boar's Glen. Being run up Glentarkie meant one bus less on returning to this forgotten end of the Ochils. For safety I was dropped off round the next bend at a place that had always interested me when driving over this way in the past: then a decayed farm, now a site reborn. On the east side of the road was a group of timber-faced houses, the Glentarkie Steading, the only place on the whole walk noteably teeming with wee birds, because of the many feeders. We may be wiping out our birds generally, by neglect and mismanagement, but then saving others by spoiling them silly at our homes. There's something not quite right in that.

There's a lot not right with our British wildlife. The UK is among the most nature-depleted countries in the world. Our whole environment is increasingly artificial. Crops are sprayed and sprayed so are starved out of wildlife, our foods are more and more pre-prepared, the ingredients listed with added chemicals. We don't notice nature's less-ness, what we have lost. We were not there, *then*, in the past, to know the richness that has gone. As a boy I roamed a landscape of birds, from hills and moors to woods and valleys. Today one is surprised by a solitary curlew or a single robin. More than 60% of rural wildlife has gone in my lifetime. Pesticides, persecution, pollution, lost habitat and climate change, means species are vanishing a hundred times faster than they would in a world sans *homo sapiens*. This is not how it was, nor how it should be, could be.

Along from the Steading was the entrance to the Scottish Offroad Driving Centre, an unusual alternative land use option. On the road a 30 m.p.h. sign took me back to day one, for there was another Walking and Cycling Friendly Road sign. However, I then left the tarmac for unknown country ahead. There was a clattering off by woodpigeons, another Houdini wren doing its usual vanishing tricks and a female pheasant went rushing off with ridiculous gait. Geese were flying over in the echoes of their own callings.

What I was on was an unexpectedly massive farm track which ran steeply down to a valley head, a spot marked Swallow Hole, which proved an overgrown pond. This might have become Swallow Whole if rash enough to walk in beyond the bullrushes. I don't think the name had anything to do with the bird, though back in the C18 and earlier, people had the notion that they did spend their winter months at the bottom of ponds. The track rose steeply on the other side, as a normal sized farm track and the reason for the big road down seemed to be that this bottom was where lorries could reach to load cattle. Right across the road was a compound of gates and stacked barriers where cattle had been corralled – and had left their mark, a coating of inescapable liquid manure. I paddled through, and prayed there would be no call to return that way.

A gurgly ditch edged the steep track up and there was a row of full-sized trees, striking individuals, personalities, including ash, chestnut, oak, Spanish chestnut, beech and sycamore. Somebody over a century ago had had an interesting sampling idea. They were all in the condition 'when trees begin to blush at their past summer opulence' and they were both natives and introductions. And why not? I wonder if people who object to introductions pause to consider their own origins. Out of curiosity, that night I looked at tree books to list our Scottish natives. They are alder, ash, aspen, bay willow, bird cherry, birch (silver and downy), hazel, holly, juniper, lime (small-leaved), oak (sessile), rowan, sallow (goat willow), Scots pine, wych elm and yew. The disputed beech I feel should be included, after all it's pollen has been found in Mesolithic sites and can't all have just blown in from pre-England. The loved and hated sycamore's original range was central Europe to the Caucasus. The horse chestnut only arrived in the C17. Larch, spruce, cedars, all the conifers, were later introductions, not a few being discovered by early Scottish plant hunters, explorers whose doings and dangers make mountaineering appear tame.

There were feeders for pheasants everywhere. The track swung right and met another, giving a view down to Strathmiglo and over to East Lomond. Any notion of cutting over fields vanished (still far too cultivated) so I turned left to follow a track up to rejoin the Glentarkie road at its summit. Initially the track was deep in mud because of cows and tractors passing. Escaping this I then had the day's surprise: in the field, on the road, and in the wood below me, were pure white pheasants. Many of them. Melanistic (black) pheasants are not rare, this opposite (leucocytic) was a complete novelty. Were they albinos? Were they a new species being reared to make easier targets for so-called sportsmen? I was so intrigued with the white pheasants, I walked past what the map named Katie Thirsty Well.

No matter, to the left the land fell away steeply in vibrant green fields and duskier woods to the Howe of Fife and the panoply of the Lomonds. Seen framed by the pillared trunks of beech trees, there was a perfect view. There was a huge ash tree as well (no sign of *chalara*) and, when I reached Glen Cottage, an old quarry was masked by copper beeches. This was the summit of the Glen-tarkie–Abernethy road. Ever willing to try my luck, rather than lose height on the Abernethy side to reach the carpark and main entrance road in to the Pitmedden Forest, I chose a short cut. The morning had started with the sort of sun that hadn't quite decided what to do with the day but, now, suddenly, decided to come out and play. Sun really sets woodlands singing. I'd enjoy the walk's second warm forest immersion.

A track was shown circling the old quarry and then stopping, but I hoped breaks in the trees (on the map anyway) might lead me to the forest road, saving time and effort. Where the track was supposed to end it continued however, and along in the direction of the break. But the track seemed to go on and on, detail not quite fitting the map and I was beginning to wonder if I had problems when, suddenly, the forest road lay in front. As if to prove all was correct, a car passed. (The track is a recognised motorable road for public use on down by The Clink to Auchtermuchty, but is in worse, pot-holed state than when I used to drive through). There were signposts but I couldn't make map agree with signs or the landscape; the map showed the onward track I wanted soon coming right up to the motorable road, so I could more or less step from one to the other, but no track appeared alongside me. Where I was was clear enough for forest-covered Drumbarrow Hill and Clamieduff lay clearly above the map's open area (too marshy for trees) and this gap ended at The Thirl Stone, whence another break might lead to my desired track. What led off along the break was a trail bike scar, which looked hopeful. As for The Thirl Stone, the only 'stone' in sight were three large boulders. Was that it? I sat on one of them to eat a jam piece and at once a robin flew in. I nearly laughed. What a chancer! But the robin ignored the possibility of a hand out and perched overhead in the sun to scrape out a small song. Wordsworth mentions a robin in fourteen poems, but as 'redbreast'. Robin only became the usual name after WW2; Britain's most popular bird.

I followed variant bike-worn tracks through rather older, more open, woodland with mature trees, the ground overgrown hummocky and the roots of the pines exposed, an unexpected sunny spot of greenery. The quiet glade duly led to the forestry track I wanted and, for the rest of the walk, map, landscape and Border kept on the best of terms.

Bike trails were everywhere, descending what looked impossible steepnesses. For all the biker trails I never encountered a bike in action while walking the Border. Does a biker dress like an American footballer? Of all sports theirs must be one of the most hazardous. Any error could be damaging, to say the least, both to rider and to steed. I've gone over the handlebars, on level tarmac, and my poor bike more or less needed rebuilding as a result, here an airy spill could end with a splat against a Scots pine. Comforting to know there are others crazier than oneself.

I soon came on a pool by another fine name, Turflundie Wood, where a wren was working through scrub. I've always loved the bird's scientific name: *Troglodytes troglodytes* and had been privileged to see the St Kilda sub species *Troglodytes troglodytes hirtensis* while on visits to Hirta, the main island of St Kilda, and the only island of the group once inhabited. St Kilda is a double World Heritage site because of the valued wildlife *and* because of the social heritage left like a shadow by her lost people.

I had my most memorable wren encounter as a youngster when camping among rhododendron bushes by Loch Quoich (there was a bullying wind). I was sitting cross-legged outside the entrance, reading, when a hyperactive, noisy wren family burst onto the scene, paying not the slightest attention to me to the extent that one of the young birds perched on my head briefly (I had a good thatch then). As boisterously as they'd arrived, they were off, through the rhoddie jungle. Moments like that give pure, unalloyed pleasure, far more, say, than when straining for experiences in a bird hide. So sad that most wildlife makes a quick exit if a human steps on stage. And today makes other exits: the most recent *Oxford Junior Dictionary* has removed words like moss, fern, acorn, conker, bluebell, magpie and otter.

There were plenty other resonant names in Pitmedden Forest: Tarduff Hill, Puries Knowe, Hill of Gettaway, Pitcairthie Hill, Craig

Sparrow, Lumbennie Hill. I sat on a pile of logs for a snack and to go through the rigmarole of having to refold a large sheet of OS 1:25,000 map. Luckily the day was near-windless (but was trying out a first attempt at winter chill). The only cyclist of the day passed.

The Border had left the Glentarkie road just below where I'd joined at the start of the day. It and ran up through farmland to go over Drumbarrow and Clamieduff Hills to reach the Thirl Stone and then followed the edge of Pitmedden Forest. For quite a long spell we were close. Had I gone cross-country earlier, one option would have been to walk the fields just outside the forest. I could now see there were gates at the fences but no gate onto the track and, continuing, fields were invaded by gorse, prehistory's barbed wire. I'd made some right decisions. The mature forest was giving very attractive walking anyway, with a pleasing tree species variety and bracken and heather and blaeberry, indicating real hill country. The map, rather weirdly just here, had Ochil Hills in bold letters, as if applying to one local place instead of being part of a range which ran all the way to Stirling.

RLS spoke of 'silence that there is among the hills' but I'm sure he was just speaking about the absence of man-made noise (logging, machinery, trains) because nature has a thousand voices at any time, whether the whirr of a beetle's wings or the bellow of an autumn stag. I recall, years ago, sitting on a bank and considering the silence was complete, but then heard a steady rasping beside me and discovered a wasp chewing at a stem of dead willowherb to glean material to make the paper to build their byke (nest). If nothing else the leaves on the trees have many voices.

I'd stopped to pick brambles from a solitary bush when these thoughts were scattered by a whole rabble of crows flying overhead – like kids let out from school. A small track led past the brambles, perhaps where roe deer trod gently through their landscape. Nature goes about its ways with so little care about mankind. Who do we think we are? Largo Law could be picked out and the Hopetoun Monument tower on Mount Hill was just visible, the Lomonds still butted in, but the world view was all Fife; Perthshire, to the north, was hidden by the forest. (Sir David Wilkie, the artist, was a Fifer and was to write about 'My Own Blue Lomonds'). A quarry, with heaps of aggregate, was passed, a notice pointing out we should be wearing hard hats, etc. A wee drop led to the romantically-named Seven Gates, a meeting place of six tracks. I met a man with an enthusiastic young dog of an eastern European breed, the dog's coat smooth and shiny as a fresh conker. The man said he had seen red squirrels but his best sighting recently had been a jay. From there on I would meet dogs and their walkers quite often. Lucky dogs. One creature I had not encountered was the fox, a surprising omission. Just one deer encountered was also surprising.

At the edge of the track I noticed three puffballs, beautifully round and white and couldn't resist giving one a little squeeze to see the puff of spores that erupted. That goes back to an early memory. As a schoolboy exploring my outdoor world I was an avid listener to a radio nature programme which was broadcast weekly to schools. Bird Man, Hut Man and others answered questions which were sent in – so I sent them some, enough that suddenly, one day the class was listening to "And this week we are just going to be answering some of the questions sent in by one boy, Hamish Brown, who lives in Dollar, a village under the Ochil Hills [*sic*] in Scotland. His first question is, 'When puffballs get rained on and the cup gets very wet and you then press them you still get a puff of spores, so how do they stay dry to do that?'" The beauty of the natural world is that there is never any end to asking questions about its wonders. Oh, the puffballs? The spores have tiny pits on the surface, like a golf ball, and this makes them stay dry, even in the wet. There were also several scatterings of fly agaric along the trackside, those red-topped toadstools out of Beatrix Potter.

From Seven Gates the track was the Border. The way I wandered about I must have alternated Fife and Perthshire regularly rather than walking with a foot in each. I smiled, recalling the excited comment of a youth as we climbed a knife-edge of snow towards the summit of Mont Blanc: "Hamish, I've got one foot in France and one foot in Italy". And that reminded me of something else: staying in a high, border hut in a mountain gap in the Pyrenees, I noticed all the Spanish litter was down the French side and all the French litter was down the Spanish side.

Just off the track lay Lumbennie Hill, 284m (*bare little hill*) which would be a satisfying high point to reach in Pitmedden Forest. Two lines of pylons went over the top, so the break shown for them would surely exist? There was a break but the ground rose steeply in an untamed jungle of bracken, bramble, heather and blaeberry; and the initial long grass approach was soaking wet. These detractions, as so often, became a spur to action. There was a trace of path. There had to be. But the path split and my left side variant fell foul of a fallen tree and became lost higher up, so I moved right to a clearer trod which on the broom-covered summit area became a good path down the other side; a puzzle, for who would come up from the empty farmland? There was one single yellow flower on the broom bush cuddling the trig point: no. 4771 (there are people who collect trig numbers!). A pair of ravens, with fine, deep Paul Robson voices, circled overhead. A patrol of oystercatchers passed – silently. The views were disappointing, foregrounds hiding the greater panorama. I was intrigued by the hill's name and later chanced on a reference to a 1291 charter being made to a Christine Lumbennie. The name is not in the current Fife phone book.

I heard voices, just below my knoll, and two women with dogs appeared on the edge of the conifers, struggling past with no interest in the trig. I'd dumped my bright yellow rucksack before heading for the hill so scampered off at once. I did not want them to come on it and, even helpfully, rescue it. My feet duly became soaked but I retrieved my rucksack while the others were still only half way down and obviously having problems. There was a yelp as one lost her footing and tried tobogganing. I was astonished to see the other had a papoose strapped on her front. They would probably find meeting anyone a bit embarrassing so I walked on, but soon stopped to have my picnic on a convenient hump of moss-covered tree stump. If they came that way, I could ask them where they had come from. I was curious. They never appeared. My fingers were stained from finding a single blaeberry bush covered in berries on the way up the hill, the first and last of the year for Fife is not really blaeberry country. I took off my trainers and wiggled my toes in the soggy socks. Considering how dry conditions had been overall (Cleish Hills day excepted) I managed to make a habit of finding wet grass. Ah, well, I thought, at least it will have removed every scent my trainers had acquired while I paddled through the cattle pens at Swallow Hole. The wood edge was quiet but better than silence I thought was the whisper of wind in the trees and the unperturbed birdsong.

Jackdaws came drifting in, two by two, and began working along the track towards me, strutting and pecking, mixing and pairing off again, so completely in their own world. I was ignored but when one pair flew off, the others rushed after. I left some crumbs, intentionally and otherwise, pulled on my wet socks and trainers and headed on, somewhat stiffly for the first minute.

That was the end of the big forest; ahead a 'confused and shaggy country' (RLS) then rolling fields. I walked along under Craigdownie and Bow Hills to the minor Auchtermuchty – Newburgh road. Below lay Lochmill Loch, with a notice warning 'Deaths have occurred at reservoirs' – and spelling out just how. (Have we strayed so far from reality that we need to be told water has dangers?) Rather unreal was finding a late feast of wild raspberries, as well as more brambles. The end of the forest also brought me back into Fife, the Border heading down deviously, west of the loch, towards the Tay, the Tavae of Ptolemy.

The deep set cluster of Lochmill buildings looked what they once were – a mill. How long ago I wondered. This area is crisscrossed with ancient roads and tracks and ravished industrial sites. On stopping to look at Macduff's Cross I suddenly recalled being involved here in a dispute decades ago when I was a director of the Scottish Rights of Way (and Access) Society. A route used for centuries ran down and along to the Tay to Carpow, where ferries crossed the River Earn as well as the Tay. Someone had blocked the right-of-way and, whenever it was cleared, did so again and again with anti-social, litigious zeal, really quite astonishing as, whenever cases like that have gone to law, the right-of-way was inevitably upheld. The most notorious case long ago was Jock's Road from Glendoll over to Braemar. The landowner took matters ultimately to the House of Lords. He not only lost the case, he lost his mansion and lands as well, for he had to sell-up to meet the expenses incurred fighting his lost cause. The mansion later became Glendoll Youth Hostel. Echoes of what I recalled were on a notice: 'Heritage Path. Old Cart Track to Macduff's Cross. Used by Roman Patrols, by Macduff fleeing Macbeth, by Queen Victoria, and as a Turnpike this path was declared a pedestrian right-of-way by the court in 1997.'

The verge had more flowers flowering than any other on my Fife crossing. There was some gorse, scabious, stiff knapweed, storksbill, straggling vetch, red campion, orpine and many I couldn't name – but surely the sharpest beauty of flowers is ours before we know their names? A family group and shaggy dog passed and Macduff's Cross seemed to be a popular about turn spot for Newburgh dog-walkers. No more sunny solitude for me.

Macduff's Cross is a striking feature but one that was, and is, 'a focal point of hotly disputed legends'. A stone-encircled mound has a huge squared-off stone in the middle. This was long thought to be the base of a cross yet Gifford notes, 'now discredited' – and yet the site has always been Macduff's *Cross.* (There is a genuine old cross near Mugdrum House). I don't think the holes said to be cupmarks are that at all. Never mind the varying views, just relish the view. And how on earth did they move the stone on site in the first place? Alas, Macduff did not leave us an autobiography and the myth-makers have had a merry time. Let me divert to tell of a first-hand experience of myth-making. I know an attractive coastal town in Morocco very well, called 'Essaouira' (pronounced Essa-wee-ra) which guide books once all explained was where the prime minister Disraeli's family came from and they gave *pages* rather than paragraphs to the story, not one word of which was true. Disraeli's father was a wealthy London man about town and the ancestry goes back to Genoa. Nothing to do with Morocco at all. But that at least could be checked.

Macduff's Cross was thought to have been a sanctuary stone for any of that clan. Anyone committing murder in hot blood could claim reprieve and consideration for his crime, this applying to relatives of Macduff to the ninth degree of relationship. The assumed cross was said to have been broken at the Reformation in 1559. A *cross* is mentioned in Wynton's c.1426 *Chronicle.*

Sceptics point out there is no hole in the stone acting as a socket to take any cross. The most interesting story tells how Malcolm, after the defeat of Macbeth, granted three requests made by Macduff: first, the family would crown the monarch; second, lead the army into battle; and third, have this privilege of sanctuary. The first two are well testified.

Sir Walter Scott and his cronies, staying with his legal friend, William Adam on one of their Blairadam Club weekends, made a long day's excursion to Newburgh, but had to ask directions for Macduff's Cross. An old tramp encountered might know, so Scott fished out a tanner and held it suggestively. "Macduff's Cross? Aye, I ken a' aboot it" the man croaked, grabbed the sixpence, and went into a wild nonsense song while waving his staff round his head and then rushing off. The party enjoyed pulling the great man's leg over the incident.

Walking on, the views suddenly, like an intercepted pass lighting up a rugger game, opened to the Tay world: complex river with its islands and banks warmed by reed beds, the rich carseland (plenty under polythene), furry lower hills and distant uphill hints of higher hills softened in the sun. Scott thought the view 'one of the finest and noblest in the world.'

The reeds and sandbanks were a novelty: nothing like them on the Forth estuary. The map gave them a curiosity of names: Wonder Bank, Reckit Lady Bank, Kerewhip Bank, the Hard, the Turk, Gilderoy Bank, Dispute Bank, Peesweep Bank. Just into Perthshire the River Earn joins the Tay, and is also tidal for a couple of miles and, anciently, a ferry crossed, Rhynd – Carpow. In the Ryhnd Churchyard I'd photographed gravestones showing ferrymen and their boats, one with a salmon on board (indicating twin occupations). The Romans had a major fort by the Tay and may well have had a bridge of boats across the river. When they departed for good they completely demolished the site.

Benches allowed me to rest my feet. A last dog of the crossing pulled his owner past, an ice-eyed huskie, Snowboy. Just one thing was missing on the Tay: spectacular bridges. The bridges from Fife to Dundee are utilitarian, lacking towers to dominate the scene as happens with the Queensferry triptych on the Forth.

Up-river an odd, hazy, movement caught my eye. The puzzling whatever suddenly blew up against the pale sky: a saturation of starlings. They flew higher and swept down in a torrent, they rose again, shimmied one way and another in a sort of oriental ballet. I sat enchanted. The term is 'murmuration'. Has anyone ever captured what must be a roar from such innumerable wings? A car stopped and a man sat staring. He must have been impressed. He turned off his blaring radio.

What is named Woodriffe Road finally descended steeply into an upper, detached part of Newburgh. Interesting, to see the various roadside gardens and what had been made of them. (One or two were simply concrete or gravel; anti-gardens.) The road crossed the railway from Fife to Perth. A two-coach train passed; unexciting; does anybody note their numbers? Heading to Perth, the train journey is exciting, for the view suddenly bursts open as the train passes above the town and all Tay is displayed. I stop reading at that point, in fact I often don't read at all on the train journey across Fife; there is just too much, too good, to not just 'sit and stare'. One sees most when afoot however, and walking after all was mankind's original, only , means of locomotion. Certainly the safest. Following the Border was not 'a daft sort of ploy' as I was told, but richly rewarding. There is no end to our discoverings.

If there was a slight touch of anti-climax on reaching Newburgh, this was due to there still being two days of the Border to walk. Stretches near the beginning of the venture, when public transport was not possible. I have however told the story in logical order, it would have been strange reading otherwise. Maximum use of the good days of autumn was essential and, on that score, I was blessed by runs of dry weather, and able to string most of the walk together in geographical order. Kincardine, I rediscovered through having to write the Fife Coastal Path book, but Newburgh I seem to have known all my life, a very satisfying place for an ending.

At the foot of Woodriffe Road the gable of the last row of cottages on the right presents an unexpected feature, with large, neat windows, on both floors, which must give fine views from the tap o' the toon. (The house was once an inn.) Across the road is the war memorial, the figure of a Black Watch Soldier, the work of Alexander Carrick, who was the sculptor of my local Kinghorn war memorial and best known for his figure of Wallace, flanking the entrance to Edinburgh Castle. Beyond, is a Victory Fountain erected, likewise, after the Great War. From here the view down the curve of High Street is inviting but I'll keep the town's description separate and, as with Kincardine and the bridges, follow a circular walk.

I turned left, past the bowling green to the town's park where an arch marks the end of the Fife Coastal Path. Having, not long before, come up from the shore to complete that fine route by walking through the arch, I thought it only right to reverse the procedure so, going through the arch I completed my circling the Border of the Kingdom of Fife. I think I so far forgot myself as to perform a little jig.

Newburgh Explored

The Border from Pitmedden Forest had skirted west of Lochmill Loch to descend above Dovens Den and Butter Well. From Craig Sparrow it was into that intense farming zone over from Macduff's cross, passing Nine Wells, Gillies Burn, Skirlbear, railway, A913, then looping round Mugdrum lands to enter the Tay. The names of the Mugdrum salmon-fishing bothies (called lodges here) are singular: Wonder Fishing Lodge, Lady Fishing Lodge, and down-river, California, Jockshole, Lovershot, Scalp, Deil-ma-Care.

Mugdrum is *muc druim* meaning pig's ridge. The Border circles round Mugdrum westwards up-river, to keep the big house and grounds in Fife (reason unknown.) The house was the home of Lord George Murray the Jacobite general in the 1745 rising, he the only Jacobite leader to come out of that debacle with credit. The mansion has had several reconstructions and is 'comfortable' rather than noteworthy. On a knoll in the policies, stands the Mugdrum Cross, alas, very worn so its panels are hard to make out; horsemen chasing stags, a boar hunt, and Celtic scrollwork. The stone for the cross came from the Lomonds. Newburgh's witches may have been burnt on the site. Permission would be needed to visit the Mugdrum Cross.

Over the South Deep lies Mugdrum Island, where in 1845, the salmon fishermen had imported Dutch cats to deal with an infestation of rats. Their bothies (lodges) line the Tay shore. High in the town there is an ice house where the salmon could be preserved before exporting – both overland and by sea. Salmon even went to Billingsgate. I've an old late C19 map which shows a ferry from Newburgh over to Port Allen in the Carse of Gowrie. A Dundee-Perth steamer called in daily in summer and vessels of 200+ tons called in to swop their cargoes to lighters which would go on up to Perth. Like Kirkcaldy, grain was a major export. Stone from local quarries went to London. One quarry remains: Clatchard Craig. The hill once had a prehistoric fort on top, guarding the route into Fife by Lindores Loch, but quarrying over the years has destroyed the site and much of the hill. On the maps the quarry shows as a large white patch. Quarrying often went hand-in-hand with mining and was as risky to limbs and lungs – in this case, pneumonoultramicroscopicsilicovolcanoconiosis, to you and me, silicosis.

With the C19 Newburgh 'rose very considerably in wealth and appearance through the industry of its people and trade on the river', Groome, 1882 notes this too, '... shops and principal dwelling-houses are of a character indicating taste and prosperity ... its situation near the Firth exceedingly pleasant ... with gardens and numerous fruit trees'. An area built southwards up the hill is named Mount Pleasant. Groome lists the town's social assets: 'Newburgh has a post office, with money order, saving's bank, insurance, and telegraph departments, a branch of the Commercial Bank, a saving's bank, agencies of 7 insurance companies, 4 hotels, a gas company (1836), waterworks (1877), a cemetery, a public library (1861), a reading room and coffee house (1881), 2 bowling clubs, a gardening society, a natural history and archaeological society, a lawn tennis club, and a young men's religious institute. A weekly corn-market on Thursday was started in 1830; and a fair is held on the third Friday of June' – quite a change from a C17 description as 'a poor country village'.

The High Street's[8] general character is Georgian vernacular, but punctuated by agreeable incidents', and is unblemished by any 1960's brutal concrete, many of the houses painted in pastel shades which remind me of similar towns in Ireland. Our perambulation of the High Street is downhill throughout and the circuit completed by returning alongside the River Tay, a nice balance with the Kincardine circuit of the bridges at the beginning. The first two colourful houses facing each other were once hotels/pubs, on the right (south) picked out in green and white, on the other in black and white, with 'rusticated quoins', a Fife speciality – quoins being the alternating long and short stones at the angles of a building. On the south are quoins in more restrained dark whinstone, with the next house light-coloured

8. Hamish imagines the reader walking through Newburgh whilst reading the subsequent paragraphs, with this book in hand!

sandstone. No 194 has a reproduction Venetian door and windows, No 192 fancy stonework. There is plenty to interest in the detail. There are passages (pends) leading through the houses in several places and all sorts of additions have been built, out-of-sight, behind, on the long strips of gardens, running up the slope southwards. These were famous for fruit growing, something linking right back to the days of Lindores Abbey whose monks were skilled horticulturalists.

Openings, or streets, on the north side of the High Street give picturesque views down to the river with it's reed beds, at St Katherine's Court seen through three arches. This is part of a 1971 reconstruction by Roland & Partners, who are based in offices in Burntisland (where I live), their offices in Rossend Castle, which they saved from dereliction. A decade later they made Newburgh's Tolbooth Close development along on the south side. In the court a stone marks the site of a chapel built by the monks, 1508, which became the first parish church, which was demolished in 1967 as beyond saving. Across Mason Street from there is the Laing Museum, inscribed as Laing Library, 1894, with 'timid tudorish detail', which, I suppose, is a polite way of the experts saying it hardly impresses, appearing a bit like a church. Inside is impressive though. Alexander Laing (1808-1894), local born, and a Newburgh banker, was a lifelong student of history. He amassed a library of some thousands of volumes which he bequeathed, along with the money to build this library, which extended to become a museum as well. Sadly, there are very limited opening hours.

One of the C18 group Nos 167 – 173 has the High Street's only remaining thatched roof, easy to overlook. (There's a blue plaque on the wall.) Hill Road runs south up the long strips area to go under the railway to houses lined along the hillside which have enviable views. Nos 83 – 87 have rare bow-fronted dormer windows on the roof. No 81, 'suave late Georgian' has fly-over steps to an iconic-pillared entrance. Beside it, Towerwell Lane is still cobbled. On the north side, the 1881 Baptist Church has been converted into a house with cheerful result. Next door, No 150, is a 1907 'Edwardian pomposity'. The Tayside Institute of 1923 is 'lumpy Scots renaissance' and is now the Community Centre and Library (n) while, south is the Roland Tolbooth Close restoration, dates on a high gable of 1888 and 1981 and a row of cottages through the pend. That side is dominated by the Town House with a clock tower and steeple, dating to 1808 (steps later), while across the road the Co-op car park gives the best view to the river from the High Street. The Bear Tavern (s) has the Earl of Warwick's stone, which bears the 'bear and ragged staff' symbol. Why, will become clear at the Abbey, from which the stone came. In it's C19 heyday Newburgh had 29 alehouses!

Over the pend between Nos 58 and 60 is the High Street's 1758 show piece, an unusually ornate marriage lintel. Not the usual simple initials and date, this was fine swank for a wealthy trader or shipowner. A globe shows navigational instruments and the names, Thomas Sanderson and Janet Williamson, alongside a ship under sail, the sun and moon above, and their motto, *Omnis Vanitas*. The south side buildings continue at a higher level with resulting attractive stairs, railings and gardens. No 32 (n) has an unusual doorway with Venetian windows above (similar windows on the south side). Candlemakers Cottage has red pantiles and, with a neighbour, are C18. When the higher level buildings end so does the High Street, with the continuation being Cupar Road. The 'lumpy Gothic' Livingstone Fountain 1887 was built to remember a John Livingstone of Musselburgh who had generously erected the original Town House and a village hall.

On the corner of Tay Street is a house, for long the George Hotel, which has a 'Doric doorway frieze, cornice and quoins' built in 1811. Across Tay Street from it is the Abbey Inn C18 (top storey C19), thankfully still an hotel – and welcome hostelry if one has completed the Fife Coastal Path. Continuing along the Cupar Road there's the Primary School (s) and Parish Church (n), the latter completed in 1906 and originally a United Free Church. The fussy decorations on tower and over the entrance porch are, apparently, 'fat, crocketed pinnacles'.

Before completing a perambulation, a few comments about the, to us, weird beliefs and superstitions of past centuries, of which Newburgh's were recorded by the antiquarian Laing, (he of the library-museum). In the early C19 a reputed witch, Jean Ford, was so regarded by local sailors that, before setting off, they would give her some form of present as a safeguard. Her landlord gave her notice on one occasion, but she went to his house where, making sure the mistress and servants observed her, began to draw signs on the ground while muttering to herself. The presumed spell worked, at least the wife's hold over her husband did, for the demand to remove was withdrawn.

Laing has many more stories of local superstitions, which even the Christian believers would follow: it was unlucky for a newborn infant to use a new cradle; a genteel way of indicating that a birth had occurred in a house was to give visitors 'butter-saps' (oatcakes crumbled and fried in butter); and 'the bairns piece' was a bit of shortbread, oatcake or whatever which was hidden in the dress of a child being carried to church for baptism and presented to the first person met on the way.

Well-attested too was the practice of lifting a suicide's coffin over the Kirk wall rather than going in through the gate, this to ensure that the next child carried in for baptism would not eventually also commit suicide.

Newburgh's most important historic site marks the natural end of the town walk, so continue along the Cupar Road to reach, and turn left onto, Abbey Road. At the junction is a filling station with the Buttercup café; seating in or out. One soon comes on the ruins of Lindores Abbey, overlooked by the Lindores Abbey Distillery which only came on stream in 2017 and is something else to see. There are tours (very popular with Germans and Japanese), a visitor centre, and refreshments, dining facilities, particularly lively on Friday evenings. Walkers completing the Fife Coastal Path are welcome to camp. The business is family run and the distillery is on the original farm steadings; the farm also owns the ruined abbey site which they maintain so attractively. Laying the foundations of the distillery proved of archaeological interest. Everything began decades earlier when finding a reference, of 1494, to a friar being commissioned by James IV to turn '8 bolls of malt into Aqua Vitae'. This inspired the idea of returning distilling to the site. While the whisky matures in the warehouse (once the old cowshed) a C21 version of Aqua Vitae, using local herbs, has been launched, which I'm sure would rejoice the heart of Friar John Cor and those who follow 500 years later.

For such a quiet site the ruins of Lindores Abbey were involved in a good slice of Scotland's bloody history. Real history fascinated me as a boy, after all, the reality was so like my reading of Henty, Haggard, Broster and Scott's *Tales of a Grandfather*.

Before going in to the site look up to the hillslope, above and beyond, where you will see the huge outline of the Earl of Warwick's 'bear and ragged staff' cut into the turf of a sloping field. Everyone has a reason why, the most likely, that the first abbot was from a minor branch of that powerful family, and may have received their sponsoring.

Look at the keystone of the entrance arch: it is made of wood. High on the inside left side of the arch you may spot a mason's mark, the personal 'signature' of the mason, proving what was his work – and he'd be paid accordingly! Inside, through little remains of the abbey, the ivy-clad ruins, the trees and grass have quite an atmosphere: a very green place, a very quiet place. It would be a crime to uncover the naked wreck of stones. There's a lingering sadness, perhaps from such wanton treatment over centuries, and from the two small stone coffins in the nave for the infant children of the founder. In the north transept is the grave of the notorious

Black Douglas (James, 9th Earl of) who gained the title on the murder of his brother William, the king (James II) being responsible. Enraged, Douglas raised a force and sacked Stirling, but the nobles, fearing Douglas powers, retaliated, and he fled to England. Thirty years on he returned to make more mischief, was captured while raiding Lochmaben and, surprisingly, was only sentenced to house arrest at Lindores Abbey where he died in his bed in 1488. At the entrance to the Chapter House is another grave with a grim story.

Here lies David, 1st Duke of Rothesay, the third son of King Robert III, the king's brother being the notorious 'Protector', the Duke of Albany (and Earl of Fife), who had his own ambitions of reigning. He had the young prince captured and shut up in Falkland Palace where he died in 1402 of dysentery (the official story) but was generally held to have been starved to death. Sir Walter Scott (yet again!) happily embellished the story in his novel, *The Fair Maid of Perth* and myth has piled on myth ever since (e.g. he was succoured by a lady offering her breast through the iron bars of his cage!). His young brother became James I, first of the six James's, few who reigned for long, until number six who ruled for an astonishing 58 years (and inherited England forby). This unchancy David was quietly buried in Lindores Abbey rather than in Dunfermline Abbey of his royal family.

One odd historical footnote I came on: in the abbey's founding charter one witness signing was a Gillascop Cambel – and that is the first record of a name which would become all too well known in Scottish history. Lindores Abbey was founded by David, Earl of Huntingdon 1178 or 1191 (sources vary) on land granted him by his brother, King William the Lion. The story goes that he was returning from the Crusades when the ship was caught in a bad storm and he vowed, if he escaped drowning, he would found a church. (That was quite the done thing among the powerful in those times.) Sir Walter Scott based the hero of *The Talisman* on Earl David. The monks were Tironensian, a stricter order of the Benedictines, and seemed to have thrived at Lindores. Newburgh, which served the abbey, prospered likewise. The abbey was built of local stone, stood by a burn which powered several mills, the sea was close for fishing, they were situated in a wood and had lands gifted to them from many benefactors. One of their investments was the effective creation of orchards (By appointment, suppliers of apples, pears, plums etc to successive King Jameses at Falkland. I noticed a big new orchard on the slope behind the distillery.) All would change at the Reformation. They were 'reformed' in the words of John Knox, in 1543, but in 1559, roused by his words while there, statues were smashed, altars overthrown and books and vestments burned. What was of value was carried off. Balmerino Abbey, along the coast, was next on this visitation.

Lindores became a lordship as so many religious establishments were, a sort of practical honours system. Sadly the abbey became little more than a quarry for Newburgh. One odd survivor from the Abbey was the bell, purchased in 1585, and now in the High Kirk of St Giles in Edinburgh.

Quite a number of earlier monarchs visited Lindores Abbey, some not in peace, like Edward I on his subjugation of Scotland, a story which had its start here. The patriot William Wallace won a battle at Black Earnside, close to the Abbey. In 1284, Alexander, the son of Alexander III died at Lindores aged twenty, his young brother David having predeceased him. This left the King with no male heir. He married a second time but, before there was any hope of producing a male heir, he was killed when he rode over a cliff one dark and stormy night, at a spot between Burntisland and Kinghorn. History turns on chance as well as intent. His daughter had married the King of Norway and their daughter, Margaret, was heir presumptuous. Sadly, 'the Maid of Norway' died on the journey to Scotland and the throne was up for grabs and manic Edward I stepped in to bang head together and say he would have Scotland. How different history would have been had Alexander not died at Lindores. The curious fact is you wouldn't be reading this had he lived.

A bracing riverside circular walk can be made from here. I've enjoyed the walk at any time of the year: along Abbey Road to Parkhill where, left, is a restored mill on the Pow Burn, wheel in place. The Fife Coastal Path comes down off the hill and then follows this Pow Burn to the River Tay, and then the river banks westwards. The layers of town look far away across the fields but that is all land reclaimed from the Tay. Reedbeds line the path awhile; they were planted in the late C18 to prevent erosion and became a big source of material for thatching, far better than rushes or marram grass; heather was also used. (I once watched a heather-thatcher at work in Glencoe village.) Rotational harvesting still takes place in a small way. The Tay reedbeds are famous as a major breeding site for bearded tits.

The path leads on to pass playing fields and sailing club and then the old harbour. The long quay with projecting piers survives and there are still a few of the old salmon cobbles in the tide-snuffing bays. On the end of one pier a gathering of black-headed gulls stood on their sturdy legs facing into the breeze. Built right over the water, starting in 1891, was the only linoleum works to rival Kirkcaldy's. The works grew from a single shed to become a huge concern before what should have been a minor financial hiccup saw the works shut down with stunning consequences for the town. I had a personal memory with the lino factory before it closed in 1987.

Our Fife school had, bit by bit, canoed from Loch Rannoch right down the Tay, and our final day was from Waukmill (opposite Luncarty) to Newburgh, in October 1963. I was leading the lads along close-to and under the high factory brick walls when a sudden jet of boiling water shot out of a pipe – and landed on the rear end of my canoe. A second earlier might have been "interesting" the lads thought.

This one-time industrial area is now grassy parkland, which can be followed (Fife Coastal Path signs) into the main park, at the top of which is the celebratory arch for Fife's coastal Border and, for me, where I celebrated, adding the overland Border. I kept notes at the time and have done some reading-up since. Old men are apt to forget things. I suppose I'm just glad to have so much to forget and, whiles, share the remembered happiness.

Not in Utopia - subterranean fields -

Or some secreted island, Heaven knows where!

But in the very world, which is the world

Of all of us – the place where in the end

We find our happiness, or not at all

                        William Wordsworth

AFTERWORD

STRANGELY, WALKING DOWN to Newburgh did feel like the true end of following the Fife Border, though two days were still to be filled in – and when they were they were just other days, nothing special. Mentally, geographically, heading down to the Tay was a consummate ending. Having done so, my priority was a refreshing coffee, only to reach the café a few minutes after closing time. The real feeling of ending came when I realised I didn't have to study forecasts so assiduously, there was no picnic to make up, no timetables to check, no alarm to be set for an inhumane hour. A brief emptiness. And then came the idea of writing about my experiences, a pressing call with my oldie's short-term memory – not the prerogative of Alan Breck Stewart with his 'grand memory for forgetting'.

The modest challenge of this peregrination had benefitted both health and fitness; remarkably so. There's nothing so boring as other peoples' ailments, so I won't repeat my conglomeration of them but, do note the positive gain from the discipline of exercise. I mention this simply to encourage anyone who feels disappointed with their present health and fitness to dream up some outdoors challenge, and do something requiring a suitable bit of push!

Head for what is naturally wilder. Forget the gym, forget social entrapment. Just go. Out there in the natural world one is not alone, one is not lonely, for one is connected with all that was, and is, and will be. That is our natural place, our rightness, our freedom; what goes for normal, urban, life is too often negative, depressing, imprisoning. Tomorrow I will not be off to walk a section of the Fife Border, I'll be out, when the tide is right, to the Black Rocks, or up the Binn to welcome a full moon rising, I'll hear curlew calling and owl hooting and know my immutable world's rewards. Whatever the effort, the Border was modest, the doing was better, and the success was better than just sitting at home on one's doup. The regrets of success are turned into memories. (Memories are dream fulfilled), endings are just beginnings for something else. In the words of the old exemplar, Captain Sir Tom Moore, 'Tomorrow is a good day.'

APPENDIX 1

Recommended Reading

The following are some of the more important books I referred to or have found particularly interesting:

Baird, B: *Shipwrecks of the Forth and Tay* 2008

Bradley, I: *The Fife Pilgrim Way* 2019. Chapter on the central mining area.

Brown, HM: *A Scottish Graveyards Miscellany*, Birlinn 2008. Comprehensive study of gravestones.

Hamish's Mountain Walk, Sandstone Press. The first continuous round of the Munros.

Hamish's Groats End Walk, Sandstone Press. The first 4 country-summits walk.

The Mountains Look on Marrakech, Whittles. The first full traverse of the Atlas Mountains.

Cooney, L & Maxwell, A: *No more Bings on Benarty* 1992. Reminiscences

Gifford, J: *Fife* 1988. Pevsner-style architectural guide.

Greenock, F: *All the Birds of the Air* 1979. Bird lore, names etc.

Glen, D & Hubbard, T: *Fringe of Gold, the Fife Anthology* 2008

Groome, FH: *Ordnance Gazetteer of Scotland* 1882. 5 large volumes.

Henderson, E: *The History of Lochoreside* 1988. Mining history.

Hutton, G: *Fife, The Mining Kingdom* 1999. Photographic study.

Laing, A: *Some Notes on the History of Newburgh* 1871

Mackay, AJG: *History of Fife and Kinross* 1890

Miller, AH: *Fife, Pictorial and Historical* 1895. 2 large volumes.

Milliken, W & Bridgewater, S: *Flora Celtica* 2004 'Plants and People in Scotland'.

Moffat, A and Brown, G: *Fife* 2019. Useful history.

Munro, D:*Loch Leven and the River Leven* 1994

Oglethorpe, MK: *Scottish Collieries* 2006. Inventory; nationalised era.

Omand, D (Edit): *The Fife Book* 2000. Comprehensive historical/topical.

Pride, GL: *The Kingdom of Fife* 1990. Architectural guide.

Snoddy, TG: *Afoot in Fife* 1950. Its post-war world.

Vickers, R: *A Dictionary of Plant Lore* 1995

APPENDIX 2

About Gravestones

THE APPEALING FOLK art on C18 gravestones first caught my interest and I still find difficulty in passing by old Kirkyards. Both Tulliallan and the 'Mausoleum' of this Border are fine examples and should not be missed. Tulliallan will need plenty of time so treat as a venue in itself; the Mausoleum is on our walk. Local enthusiasts restored the Tulliallan Kirkyard, seeing broken stones were repaired, new bases made, fallen stones lifted, the surfaces cleaned, and inscriptions and symbols recorded, a mammoth task, completed in 1997. William Wolsey and William Anderson of the Kincardine Local History Group were the restorers, making the site one of the most notable in the country. Of necessity, in these vandal-rife days, the site is kept locked but a key and site inventory can be had from Marco's Kitchen, on the corner at the start of Kirk Street.

I recommend having a coffee there first to have a look at the inventory. Every stone is described, every name, every art work, every trade, every admonitory rhyme. ('My glass is run and yours is running/ Mind death for judgements coming'.) They report, too, that one stone was 'upright, but upside down' and many of the masons had their own quirks; not being seamen they often show ships under sail with a flag flying against the wind! Tulliallan is particularly rich in nautical associations, from a stone showing a man felling a tree, shipwrights at work, complete hulls, and the proud pictures of owners' vessels under sail. Some ships are even named. Ship masters graves had navigational instruments shown, Merchants the symbol 4 (or reversed), suggesting the four corners of the world. Much trade was with the Baltic where ports froze up in winter and traders took on other winter work on the land, as a smith for example, and their stones may show both trade symbols.

But before going on further about the trade stones, a word about what appears on old gravestones generally. A first look can be a bit overpowering. What does all the symbolism mean? Naturally, the majority of stones have religious symbols and these break down into two groups: symbols of mortality and symbols of immortality.

The symbols of mortality are all the skeletons, skulls and bones, coffins, hour-glasses, handbells or Father Time with his scythe, all obvious but with many subtleties (an hourglass implies time is running out but one lying sideways means time has run out!). The symbols of immortality make up the largest contribution (after all that was what was hoped for) and the most frequently seen are the winged 'faces' at the top of stones. These are not angels but a symbol of a spirit winging to heaven. Angels may be shown blowing the trumpets of the resurrection, or offering a crown of life, and then there are figures rising at the last day or the tree of life or some symbol like a heart.

Rarer (none at Tulliallan), are the portrayings of Bible stories, either showing Adam and Eve, or Abraham about to sacrifice his son. Notable sites at Logierait, Grantully, Abernyte and Lundie.

Always look on both sides of gravestones: one may be mainly text and the other have the symbols, of trade in particular. I defy anyone not to be captivated at the trade symbols, particularly rich at Tulliallan. The sea connection has already been mentioned but other allied trades appear too, like net or rope makers. Fishermen and ferrymen have sea connections too. A sailor may have an anchor shown (upside down shows 'anchored above'). A crown over hammer is for hammermen, a guild of those working in metal which can be a watchmaker or gunsmith, this last probably why the crown appears. The crown only appears otherwise over the symbol of cordiners (shoemakers); why, a puzzle.

One of the commonest symbols, Tulliallan and everywhere, is the sock and coulter, the two parts of the then primitive plough, when working on the land was still the largest occupation. They often have a second symbol for those tying down two occupations. The service industries are noted: a Baxter (baker) with loaves on paddle ready for the oven (in one case only, a rolling pin), Fletcher (butcher) with his various tools, Candlemaker, Tailor (goose iron, wide scissors etc), Glover, Weaver (from showing a shuttle to a man sitting at a loom), Gardener (tools just as we have them today), Carter, Shepherd, and Masons (mell and chisels).

Not all of these will be seen at Tulliallan (and there are many more) but the Inventory lists those that are. My book *A Scottish Graveyard Miscellany* illustrates many of these, besides mentioning many other gravestone topics: Covenanters, Body-snatchers, Disasters etc. I've even photographed Bart Simpson on a stone!

I also describe the large topic of what is written on stones. Some of it is extraordinary. Racist? A stone in the USA, 'To the memory of Sam L Frame, who during his life shot 89 Indians whom the Lord delivered into his hands, and who was looking forward to making up his hundred when he fell asleep in Jesus'. Stupid? A stone in Shetland, to 'Donald Robertson, d. 1848, aged 63 years ... His death was much regretted which was caused by the stupidity of Lawrence Tulloch of Clothister who sold him nitrate instead of Epson Salts by which he died in the space of 5 hours after taking a doze of it'. I have come on two stones where people are recorded as dying on April 31st, and a youth, Born 1859, Died 1840.

Greyfriars Graveyards all seem to have good displays, Perth Greyfriars has many under cover and described, Dundee Greyfriars is The Howff and Edinburgh Greyfriars is the busiest, thanks to the association with Greyfriars Bobby.

ACKNOWLEDGEMENTS

My thanks to the following who helped in various practical ways:

Howard Andrew, Richard and Edith Cormack, Roger Diggins, George Mc Quitty, Andrew Snowball and Simon Payne; Ros Moffat who turned an unruly text into useable draft; to Rachel Nordstrom, Jane Campbell and Laura Brown in turn, from the St Andrews University Library Special Collections for accessing my photographic archive and scanning illustrations used in the book, to Robert Dawes and Adrian Snowball who, later on, travelled with me to take most of the photographs and to Shutterstock for grsnting us licence to use a photograph of the Bunnet Stane. Thanks also to Heather Moncur for permission to use her father, Douglas Fraser's poem *'The Quiet Glen'* from his collection *The Landscape of Delight;* to Ian Crofton for the quote from his *Walking the Borders* (Birlinn 2014); to Revd. Dr. Ian Bradley for using material from his informative *The Fife Pilgrim Way* (Birlinn 2019); to Cathy Watt and Neon Productions for her late husband, John Watt's, joyful song *'The Keltie Clippie'.* As ever I am indebted to my local Burntisland Library and Central Library, Kirkcaldy in finding books or using their fine research facilities. I owe a further debt to Tom Johnstone for his patient editorial work, to my nephew Colin Brown for computer skills and to Diana Diggins and Brian Kerr at Eventispress, who took on the publishing of this book.